Eryl Davies has written a painfi
It is a sad reality that some chui
of the reality of domestic abuse.
part of the problem. So it is with
Eryl shares the accounts of suffe
of churches to respond to the evil that is domestic abuse. For
some Christians this will be a real eye opener, but all who
read this book will find it moving, challenging and providing
valuable guidance.

Writing with patience and care, Eryl acknowledges the
courage of sufferers, and brings scripture to bear on the sin of
domestic abuse. Helpful pastoral advice is offered, and a clear
biblical understanding of marriage presented. The chapter
on divorce is particularly stimulating. This book should be
required reading for all church leaders, everywhere.

Philip Swann
Pastor, Llanelli Free Evangelical Church,
Pastoral Theology lecturer, Evangelical Movement of Wales

Dr Eryl Davies has given us a book that is desperately needed
in the church, and one which has been written by the request of
those who have suffered for years, often in silence. For too long
the church has kept quiet about domestic abuse, which has led
to both confusion and pain. Dr Eryl Davies has a rare blend of
great theological mind and genuine pastoral heart, and in this
book he has worked with those who have experienced domestic
abuse, to create a book that blends personal accounts, biblical
insight, and pastoral wisdom. I wept as I read sections of the
book, and was forced to think deeply about what I believed
and taught. This book is a must read for church leaders and
members alike, and both those who are suffering and those
who are supporting. I pray that this book would help many to
find safety and love in the church.

Jonathan Thomas
Pastoral Dean, Union School of Theology,
Pastor, Cornerstone Church, Abergavenny, Wales

This book about the *Hidden Evil* of domestic abuse in 'Christian' marriages, written at the request of several survivors of abuse, is a must-read for all in church leadership, especially in Bible-believing churches, and perhaps particularly in independent churches. It should also be read by as many Bible-believing Christians as possible.

The book was written 'at the request of several survivors of abuse' and out of significant, personal pastoral engagement that Dr Davies has had with victims of often atrocious abuse, as well as out of his detailed research and personal, prayerful wrestling with the truths of Scripture on the matter of marriage, separation and divorce.

This is a deeply disturbing book. One cannot but weep at the depths of pain and suffering experienced by the likes of 'Charlotte,' a pastor's wife (chapter 7), typical of so many victims of abuse by 'Christian' spouses, who writes: 'The evangelical world had supported my husband wholeheartedly without knowing the facts.' Leadership in the evangelical world needs to waken up, and in some cases will need to implement Dr Davies' suggestions 'as a matter of urgency.'

Hector Morrison
Principal, Highland Theological College, Scotland

Davies wakes us up to the disturbing reality that the church is not immune to the horrors of domestic abuse – whether physical, psychological, emotional, spiritual or sexual. Yet this is not something the church knows how to handle. Davies gives us the data and tools we need to dig our heads out of the sand and help those in danger!

Natalie Brand
Lecturer and research supervisor, Union School of Theology, Wales,
Author of several books, including *Prone to Wander* and *Complementarian Spirituality*

Eryl Davies

HIDDEN EVIL

A Biblical & Pastoral Response
To Domestic Abuse

CHRISTIAN
FOCUS

Copyright © D. Eryl Davies 2019

paperback ISBN 978-1-5271-0331-3
epub ISBN 978-1-5271-0371-9
mobi ISBN 978-1-5271-0372-6

10 9 8 7 6 5 4 3 2 1

First published in 2019
by
Christian Focus Publications Ltd,
Geanies House, Fearn, Ross-shire,
IV20 1TW, Great Britain.

www.christianfocus.com

Cover and Interior Design by MOOSE77

Printed and bound
by Bell & Bain, Glasgow

CONTENTS

Foreword

I count it a great privilege to write this foreword. I know of no one better equipped to address this urgent and disturbing problem than Eryl Davies. Dr. Davies brings to the task an immense wealth of pastoral experience extending over the past sixty years, besides skill as a Biblical exegete, great learning, and considerable theological acumen. He continues to this day deep in his studies and in dispensing what *The Book of Common Prayer* describes as 'ghostly counsel and advice.'

The problem of domestic abuse is acute, the stories that follow are heart-wrenching; lives ruined, careers destroyed, children permanently damaged, all through cruel abuse, whether physical, psychological, financial, sexual, or spiritual. Sadly, sometimes Christian ministers have been involved, whether as the abuser or the abused. Too often this catalogue of misery has been aided and abetted by conservative evangelical churches. Scripture has been wrongly interpreted, slanted to insist that battered women return to their abusive husbands and submit, to be beaten up further. Meanwhile, men have been programmed to endure constant psychological assault in silence, while women live in fear that few will believe their story. Sometimes the victim's patience runs out, with devastating consequences.

Dr. Davies addresses a range of situations, always with discretion and sensitivity. He highlights the glaring deficiencies in church leadership, the lack of knowledge, wisdom, and Christian sensitivity. His conclusions may unsettle some who have not considered these matters before. He addresses the views of divorce and remarriage commonly held by evangelicals, strongly affected as they are by the Roman Catholic and Anglican attitudes that regard divorce as effectively forbidden. A minister I know well was put through a nasty divorce some years back and asked counsel from a range of evangelical leaders in the UK; he was given as many opinions as the people he had canvassed. Amidst this appalling confusion and ignorance, Dr. Davies expounds the Biblical grounds for divorce, reinforced by the classic Protestant and Reformed teaching. This needs to be pondered and taught once again.

Among the narratives that follow are lessons for the churches in Britain and elsewhere. Dr. Davies wisely points to ways forward to overcome toxic attitudes, to help victims of abuse (men as well as women), and to guide pastoral care. He recognizes that few pastors have the specialized gifts or knowledge to handle situations of abuse themselves and so indicates ways that appropriate help can be obtained.

All Christians should read the Bible; I recommend anyone studying theology to become familiar with Calvin's *Institutes*. Beyond that I have never suggested that a book be read by everyone. However, so pressing is this matter – it is far more common than you may think – that I urge all in positions of church leadership to take up this book and read. Failure to come to grips with this issue at this time and place will be little short of a dereliction of pastoral duty.

Robert Letham

Professor of Systematic and Historical Theology, Union School of Theology
Formerly Senior Minister, Emmanuel Presbyterian Church, Wilmington, Delaware,
USA (1989-2006)

Preface

Researching and writing this book has been demanding, but meeting and sharing with those who have suffered domestic abuse has been a privilege. Their sharing has been stressful for them, with some relating their experiences of abuse for the first time. Some have had to cope with waves of conflicting emotions, flashbacks, guilt and fears when, and also after, describing the atrocious abuse they experienced over long periods. Their openness and trust have been refreshing but particularly their desire as believers to please the Lord, even in difficult circumstances. My debt to them is considerable and it is a privilege to make their voices heard through this book. It is at the request of several survivors of abuse that this book has been written, though it has been a long time in preparation! Not all the survivors of domestic abuse I know and shared with have felt able or ready, for different reasons, to share their experience of abuse in this book. I respect their decision and appreciate their support as well as their prayers.

SUGGESTIONS

In addition to the personal stories being told here, I draw your attention to their suggestions for improving pastoral care in churches for those suffering domestic abuse. These valuable suggestions are included mostly in later chapters and churches will find them stimulating. For some churches, these suggestions need to be implemented as a matter of urgency.

PRAYER

I am indebted to those Christians who prayed for me while writing this book. Prayer support has been so necessary as well as encouraging, for the going has been tough at times and daunting, but the Lord has answered prayer. Ongoing prayer is needed too, for all who have suffered domestic abuse, because the pain, anguish and consequences of domestic abuse continue for years, long after separation from the abuser. Nor should we forget in prayer the abuser and the needs which he or she has but may not recognise.

RESULTS

There are two results I would love to see from the publication of this book. One is for those who have been, or remain, in abusive relationships to be encouraged personally, listened to, accepted and welcomed lovingly in their churches. They must not feel isolated and left on the fringe of church life. They need to be loved and cared for by the whole church. A second result I covet is for us as Christians, whoever we are, to express even more practically, the glorious love of the triune God in our relationships. It is in the family unit first that this divine love needs to be radiated and promoted. In this respect, husbands have a huge responsibility and privilege to love 'as Christ loved the church' while wives can also model the church's submission to Christ by their gracious attitude to their husbands.

To the triune God, Father, Son and Holy Spirit be all the glory.

Eryl Davies
Cardiff, Wales,
Summer 2018

PART 1
INTRODUCTION

1. Challenges

There are challenges facing readers of this book! One challenge is to engage with its contemporary and biblical message concerning the distressing and urgent problem of domestic abuse, against the canvas of the global abuse and trafficking of women and girls, men and boys. Here is a global problem which shows no sign of improvement. Another challenge will be reading uncomfortable sections where victims relate their painful experiences of domestic abuse. These victims, both male and female, need to be listened to and cared for; their children, too, who witness the abuse – often for years – need our support and prayers. Their stories may be a huge challenge for you to reflect on. A further challenge to readers is that victims of domestic abuse in a 'Christian' marriage often report that they find little support or understanding from their church leaders and members. No one seems to care. Admittedly, caring for victims can be costly, time consuming and long-term so that church leaders may feel they cannot give the time, or do not understand the problem, or know the way forward. Whatever the reasons, generally pastoral care for victims of domestic abuse has been, and remains inadequate, but too often non-existent. That is a pressing challenge.

AIMS

There are five aims which control the content and purpose of the following chapters. The first aim is to provide a global background illustrating the fact that domestic violence is only one aspect of a worldwide problem of human abuse and cruelty. This is important because globally the dignity and worth of humans is totally ignored by some people in order to exploit women and men, boys and girls; such exploitation has the purpose of satisfying personal lust, promoting slave labour and sex-trafficking for financial gain and obtaining control over people. Against this background we will begin to focus on domestic abuse from chapter three. The second aim is to define and describe domestic violence/abuse particularly in the West, and to highlight attempts made by governments and others to address the problem. There are encouraging developments but much more needs to be done. A third aim brings us to the heart of this book, namely, registering and discussing the fact of domestic abuse in some Christian families. This problem is surfacing as more individuals feel free to seek help. Children too in families where there is, or has been, domestic abuse tend to be overlooked and they are calling for churches to appreciate their plight and distress in such situations. All stories of domestic abuse are heartbreaking so pastoral support and compassion are urgently needed.

CHURCHES

The Christian families I am referring to are attached to Bible-believing churches. The churches are mostly independent, often affiliated to a wider network or association of churches and they may be within a formal Protestant, sometimes Presbyterian or Baptist, denomination. What is common to these churches, despite differences in church polity and location, is a faithful adherence to the Bible as their supreme authority in all matters of faith and practice. For numerous reasons, churches may be unaware of domestic abuse in their community. Or they may not believe the victim's story or feel ill-equipped to deal with the problem. This third aim draws attention to a hidden problem and crime in some families. A fourth aim seeks to describe the suffering of Christians who are or have been abused by marriage partners. At their request, I am expressing their cries for help, their frustration, questions, disappointment, loneliness, and even isolation. Often, victims complain they do not seek pastoral help because they fear no one will believe them or they doubt whether church leaders will keep their information confidential.

FEAR

Some women report they cannot disclose their experiences of abuse for fear of reprisal, including the fear of children being taken from them. Many victims feel confused because of mixed feelings of guilt and loyalty to an abuser. Some of their stories as well as their suggestions for pastoral support will be shared in later chapters. The book's final aim is to offer pastoral help to churches and to individuals who suffer domestic abuse or its effects. Difficult questions need to be grappled with, such as the biblical grounds for the victim seeking a divorce or should one stay permanently with a violent partner, despite the dangers? Should the police be involved? And what if legal proceedings are taken against the abuser? What support and encouragement can churches give both to the victim and the abuser, including their children? We need to interpret and apply the biblical text responsibly and compassionately in answering these questions.

INVOLVEMENT

After being urged by a group of churches to research the subject of domestic abuse in Christian families, I was introduced online – and unexpectedly – to a small, confidential network of Christian women in the United Kingdom who had suffered abuse from their husbands. I appreciated their trust and willingness to share their experiences with me for purposes of research. Three common threads in their stories stood out and troubled me. The first thread in common was that their abusive husbands were professing Christians with prominent positions in church life and leadership. A second thread in their stories was that they had received no pastoral support or encouragement in their churches. They were either ignored or not believed. They all feared that in telling anyone about their situation that their husbands would punish them more and their children would be at greater risk. That was the third thread in their stories that appalled me. These women were desperate for help. Providentially they were eventually able to leave their husbands with the appropriate external support from professionals, one of whom was a Christian who had herself suffered domestic abuse. Along with their children, they were safe from abusive 'Christian' husbands but the road to recovery and stability for them has been long and challenging.

Despite their initial encouragement, however, my research made slow progress, due to pressures of work. Pastors or church elders contacted me at intervals seeking advice concerning a church member or adherent caught up in domestic abuse. One pastor believed the victim's story but his church elders refused to believe the victim, even threatening to divide the church if it was taken further. What was he to do? Often in these situations, the abuser is a faithful member, even a gifted and popular church worker and preacher. As I met other individuals in abusive relationships, a similar pattern emerged and I am especially indebted to two ladies who visited our home on occasions requesting me to write and speak publicly on the subject to church leaders. One lady had herself suffered horrific abuse from her 'Christian' husband and both ladies continue to encourage women in their churches/localities who are in abusive relationships. Both report that in churches known to them, women victims are not being helped. I am grateful for their prayers and their challenge for me to speak and write about Christians suffering domestic abuse but I also apologise to them and others that it has taken so long to respond to their pleas to write on this subject.

MALE VICTIMS

Pastorally it is mostly female victims of domestic abuse I have been in contact with but there are a handful of Christian men I know, unknown to one another, who have suffered, or continue to endure, considerable psychological, emotional and verbal abuse from their wives. I know their stories. For two of them their way of coping with the situation is to be engaged in demanding work situations with long working hours and travel. One man in a different situation will share his painful and more subtle experience of abuse and its aftermath in a later chapter. I want to register at the outset, therefore, that men can suffer domestic abuse from their wives/partners. Just like female victims, the abuse experienced by men can be physical but more often it is psychological, emotional, financial and verbal. Such abuse is often relentless and vicious but hidden from outsiders. Yes, more women than men suffer domestic abuse, yet men are sometimes victims rather than abusers. This fact is often overlooked with men finding it difficult for their story to be believed by the police, social agencies, courts and even churches. As background to our discussion of domestic abuse, we will look at the wider and global challenge of abuse in the next chapter.

2. A Global Challenge

There are compelling reasons for referring to global abuse in a book devoted to domestic abuse in churches. For example, each year an International Day for the Elimination of Violence against Women is observed which challenges us to think globally concerning the problem. The United Nations describes violence against women as a global pandemic. One regional newspaper in the United Kingdom reports: 'The problem is incredibly serious, for the world, and for Wales'.[1] Furthermore, we are reminding ourselves that domestic abuse is only one important aspect of the more extensive and variegated abuse which affects all countries. Again, churches in the West need to be informed concerning the varied forms of global abuse. We must not be insular and exclusively concerned with abuse in our own country and churches. There is also the disturbing fact that these global forms of abuse are present in all Western countries, including the United Kingdom; in fact, the U.K. Government is committed to eradicating these forms of abuse but the problem is extensive, secretive as well as persistent. Our prayers and active support for these government measures are important and necessary. There are also examples on our doorstep! Finally, churches have the opportunity to support and encourage Christians and their churches, especially in

1   *Western Mail*, 'Violence against Women Incredibly Serious', Saturday 25 November 2017, p. 26.

Third World countries where such abuse is rife, often affecting people in their own families, churches and neighbourhoods.

GLOBAL ABUSE

Alongside domestic abuse in countries, there are other related abuses worldwide which we need to identify. For example, the unprecedented mass movement of people across Europe from Africa, Asia and South America has recently aggravated problems of abuse in general in Western Europe. In escaping from poverty, famine and wars, migrants have been subjected to abuse or have themselves perpetrated abuse, some creating powerful sex and slave labour rings. Amnesty International reports that female migrants face physical assault, exploitation and sexual harassment on their journey through Europe and they lack support or protection.[2] The Press warned that unaccompanied young refugees in Europe were 'at risk from organised criminal gangs'[3], intent on forcing younger women and girls into prostitution and slave labour. The United Nations Refugee Agency also warned that refugee women on the move in Europe are at risk of sexual and gender-based violence.[4] Such abuse is perpetrated by fellow refugees, smugglers, male relatives and even European police. The European Union Committee claim that the refugee crisis in Europe is the greatest humanitarian challenge to have faced the European Union since its foundation and unaccompanied children are at the forefront of the crisis[5]. Interestingly, the United Nations

2   'Female refugees face physical assault, exploitation and sexual harassment on their journey through Europe', 18 January 2016. https://www.amnesty.org/en/latest/news/ Last accessed 8 November 2018.

3   *The Guardian,* 'Unaccompanied Young Refugees in Europe at Risk from Criminal Gangs', Sunday 1 November 2015.

4   'Refugee women on the move in Europe are at Risk, says UN', 20 January 2016. http://www.unhcr.org/uk/news/latest/ Last accessed 8 November 2018.

5   European Union Committee: Second Report of Session 2016-17, HL Paper 34: 'Children in Crisis: unaccompanied migrant children in the EU.'

highlighted this abuse especially from 1979[6] in advocating women's human rights but implementation has been variable.[7]

EXTENT OF ABUSE

In *Half The Sky: How to change the world*[8] authors Nicholas Kristof and Sheryl WuDunn, provide a chilling exposure of the abuse of women and girls worldwide, including sex trafficking, female genocide, genital mutilation, honour killings, early and forced marriages. They appeal to American Christians to include the rescuing of African women from these cruel forms of abuse alongside their programme for saving the lives of unborn babies. In 2015, Elaine Storkey developed this subject in her *Scars Across Humanity: Understanding and Overcoming Violence Against Women.* One reliable Egyptian source reported, for example, that Egypt may be top of the league in terms of violence on women, including domestic abuse. A former UN Women Executive Director affirms that 'up to seven in ten women continue to be targeted for physical and/or sexual violence in their lifetime' while '603 million women live in countries where domestic violence is still not a crime'.[9]

---

6   The UN General Assembly accepted the Convention on the *Elimination of All Forms of Discrimination Against Women* which has since been referred to as an international bill advocating women's human rights.

7   See also the UN Secretary-General's study: *Ending Violence against Women: From Words to Action (2006),* which influenced more governments and political/social/ humanitarian agencies to address the problem with greater urgency. Also, UN Department of Economics and Social Affairs (2010) *Handbook for Legislation on Violence against Women; 2012.* The UN Assistance Mission in Afghanistan produced a disturbing account of abuse in the country but encouraging call for further action (see *Still a Long Way to Go: Implementation of the Law on Elimination of Violence against Women in Afghanistan*). Also, in 2010 the *UN Chronicle* carried a compelling article under the title, 'United Nations Agencies Forward Together in the Response to Violence Against Women'. UNESCO, the World Health Organisation and the Council of Europe have helpful resources on various aspects of the subject.

8   Kristof, D. N., and Wudunn, S., *Half the Sky: How to change the world* (New York/ London: Knopf/Hatchette, 2009).

9   Storkey, E., *Scars Across Humanity: Understanding and Overcoming Violence Against Women (*London, SPCK, 2015) p. 77.

HUMAN TRAFFICKING

The slave trade officially ended two hundred years ago but in 2018 an estimated 40.3 million people were enslaved worldwide[10]. Women and girls make up 71 per cent of all victims with one in four victims being children. Half of all victims of modern slavery are in debt bondage. Frequently slavery takes the form of domestic servitude in private homes where there is psychological and physical, including sexual, abuse. 'Modern slavery' is a term used within the United Kingdom and defined within the Modern Slavery Act 2015. The U.K. Government understands human trafficking to include sexual exploitation, forced labour, domestic servitude, organ harvesting, forced labour, child exploitation, forced marriage and illegal adoption. In July 2011 the Conservative and Liberal Democrat Coalition Government published its *Human Trafficking Strategy* policy document expressing 'a renewed focus on prevention overseas' and at home. The Government 'seeks to strengthen intelligence-gathering and-sharing through the new National Crime Agency'. Police in England and Wales recorded 2,255 modern slavery offences in the year ending March 2017 which represented a 159 per cent increase on the previous year. Human trafficking remains a global reality. In 2014 the *UN Global Report on Trafficking in Persons* identified a minimum of 124 countries where human trafficking exists and is operated by people from many different cultures and countries. The *Global Slavery Index 2013* suggested the total figure of trafficked victims was near to thirty million.[11] For example, trafficking is a major problem in the north of Vietnam while in Nepal about 20,000 young girls from poor areas are trafficked into brothels or domestic

---

10   Council on Foreign Relations (CFR): *Modern Slavery: An Exploration of its root causes and the human toll.* A CFR Information Guide.

11   Storkey, p. 99.

slavery and sent as far as the Middle East. Due to China's strict one-child policy in recent decades, there is an inadequate number of spouses available for marriage so to meet the needs of millions of men there is a prosperous, organised trafficking of girls across South East Asia into China who are forced into marriage or prostitution. These girls come from countries including N.E. Myanmar, Mongolia, North Korea, Russia, Burma and Laos. Near the borders of Nepal, Burma and Bangladesh, Calcutta 'is a hub for the regional slave trade', reports Hugh Tomlinson. Police raids frequently discover young women kidnapped from neighbouring states together with Indian girls going in the other direction. 'It's so easy to sell a child here,' reports one young lawyer. Children, however, are more often kidnapped and forced into prostitution. That was the experience of Indian police when they raided a house on the outskirts of Calcutta early in 2018 and found over a dozen girls, some as young as twelve, crowded into a small, dark room. India has the highest number of under-age sex workers in the world, supplied by a booming child-trafficking industry. An estimated 1.2 million children are involved in the sex trade in India while their captors are rarely punished.[12]

FORCED MARRIAGE

Forced Marriage (FM) of both women and men is also a serious abuse of human rights. The pressures on individuals involved in FM are physical by means of threats, finance, violence or/and rape, often with emotional pressure, suggesting the family will be shamed if FM does not proceed. In the United Kingdom, FM includes individuals and families from the Indian sub-continent, countries like Pakistan, India and Bangladesh[13].

---

12 Tomlinson, Hugh, 'From our Correspondent', *The Times*, Monday March 26, 2018, p. 34.

13 In 2005, the Government's Home Office and Commonwealth Office established a Forced Marriage Unit (FMU) to identify, support and advise victims but to

Research in 2017 by the Save the Children charity and the World Bank discovered that over 20,000 girls are married daily and approximately 7.5 million girls are married illegally each year.[14] The disconnect between national, cultural, tribal and religious laws facilitates child marriage. Both the Save the Children charity and the World Bank have called for all countries to make the age of eighteen the legal marrying age yet children under the age of fifteen account for 44 per cent of child victims of forced marriage.[15]

VIOLENCE

More generally, it is reported that one in three women worldwide continue to experience physical or sexual violence, mostly by an intimate partner.[16] The World Health Organization[17] regards violence against women, especially intimate partner violence, as a major public health problem and the violation of women's human rights; this is a fact we need to bear in mind when considering domestic abuse both in the U.K. and in our churches. These facts indicate that domestic violence/abuse occurs daily in the homes of millions of people worldwide. Before leaving this global perspective on abuse, reflect on the following figures:

- Worldwide, more than 700 million women living today were married as children.
- Globally, approximately 38 per cent of the murders of women are committed by a male intimate partner.

---

date convictions are few in number.

14 *The Guardian*, 'More than 20,000 underage girls marry illegally each day, claims study', 11 October 2017. https://www.theguardian.com/lifeandstyle/2017/oct/11/ Last accessed 8 November 2018.

15 Council on Foreign Relations: *Modern Slavery: An exploration of its root causes and the human toll*. A CFR Information Guide.

16 'UN Women: Facts and Figures: Ending Violence Against Women.' www.unwomen.org/en/what-we-do/ Last accessed 8 November 2018.

17 World Health Organization: Violence Against Women: Intimate Partner and Sexual Violence Against Women. Fact Sheet: Updated November 2016.

- 43 per cent of women in twenty-eight European Union Member States have experienced some form of psychological violence by an intimate partner. Of those who seek help, less than 10 per cent turn to the police for assistance.
- Approximately 15 per cent of women aged between 15-49 in Japan and 71 per cent of women in Ethiopia in the same age group reported physical/psychological violence by an intimate partner.
- The situation in France is 'worrying'. It is one of thirteen countries where 20.2 per cent of women report physical or sexual violence by a partner. One woman dies every two days in France due to this abuse.
- 64,500 of 215,000 violent sexual crimes, including rape, recorded across the European Union in the year to March 2017 were in England and Wales, compared with 34,300 in Germany.[18]

The next chapter focuses more narrowly on domestic abuse in the United Kingdom and America.

---

18 European Union official statistics. See also *The Guardian*, 23 November 2017 and Alan Travis's article: 'England and Wales police record highest number of violent sexual crimes in EU'. The Office for National Statistics say that the majority of victims did not report their abuse to the police.

3. A Contemporary Challenge

It has been described as one of the momentous cultural moments during 2016 in the United Kingdom. The reason? Millions of people were absorbed with developments in the trial of Helen Titchener who was accused of stabbing husband Rob after his sustained campaign to abuse and control her. To the public, Rob was a charmer, a doting husband, supportive, but very few saw beyond the mask. They had no idea what he was doing to Helen in their home – controlling, threatening, assaulting, humiliating and isolating her. Helen became more and more desperate then suddenly one day she stabbed her husband in self-defence. Helen pleaded not guilty. And after months of waiting and speculation by the public in anticipation of the trial and eventual verdict, the jury in court accepted her plea, declaring her not guilty.

CONTEMPORARY

I hasten to add that this story is fictional. It was dramatized in the popular BBC Radio 4 programme, *The Archers,* a story which continued for a two-and-a-half-year period until 2016. Millions of people tuned in as this domestic situation deteriorated and ended in court. In fact, a special episode was extended to one hour for the first time in the sixty-five-year history of this radio programme. The story stimulated considerable debate and discussion in the nation. Fiction – yes, but the situation and details described in the programme are real and contemporary. The script writers consulted widely with those who had been abused domestically and with those having responsibility in helping both victims and abusers. This radio programme depicted what is actually happening in the real world. Domestic abuse is certainly not fiction. What this radio programme achieved in the United Kingdom was to alert more middle-class people to the problems and reality of domestic abuse. Previously, some TV 'soaps' like *Coronation Street* and *Eastenders* had highlighted the problem, possibly reaching more working-class viewers. Domestic abuse, therefore, is a reality.

On average, two women per week in the United Kingdom die as a result of domestic violence by an intimate partner and annually about one quarter of a million women live in fear of domestic violence. Domestic abuse, therefore, is not something to laugh or joke about. That was what the Australian politician Alexander Downer discovered in 1994. Playing on the words of his party's election slogan, 'The Things that Matter', he jokingly remarked that their domestic violence policy could be called 'The Things that Batter'. The joke received wide publicity across the nation and it was not well received although Downer himself went on to become Australia's longest serving Minister for Foreign Affairs. He learnt his lesson: domestic abuse is not a joke. Acknowledging that many more women than men suffer domestic abuse, one national newspaper in the United Kingdom draws attention to the fact that the abuse of males by partners is also 'a prevalent problem'[1] and we need to discuss this before proceeding further.

---

1   *The Telegraph*, 'Why will no one fund male domestic abuse charities?', Jonathan Wells, 26 November 2015.

MEN AS VICTIMS

We have already emphasised that men can and do suffer domestic abuse from their partners. In fact, one in six men experience domestic abuse. The background to this aspect of the problem takes us back to the early 1970s. It was in this period that domestic abuse became a political issue in some Western countries, then in 1971 the first refuge for abused women and their children was opened in Chiswick, England. The founder of the refuge was Erin Pizzy. Interestingly, reflecting later on the refuge, she wrote: 'of the first 100 women who came to the refuge, 61 were as violent or as violent prone as the men they had left'.[2] Government and public policies from the 1970s began to provide significant financial support for victims of domestic abuse but this was almost entirely directed towards the protection and support of female victims. On the other hand, academic and government research established that there are significant levels of female aggression and abuse of an intimate partner. In fact, women initiate the abuse against their intimate partner in one quarter of the abuse incidents and approximately one third of those injured in domestic abuse cases are men.

One of the consequences of official policy and funding has been to give a low profile to male victims of domestic abuse. Male victims are also unlikely to be believed by the police/social workers with so many male victims not reporting the abuse to the police. If they do report the abuse, surveys reveal that about one in five male victims are arrested rather than the abuser! In Australia, one official statistic[3] revealed that almost one in three victims of intimate partner abuse are male;

---

2   PARITY: *Male Victims of Domestic Abuse*, p. 1. The campaign group PARITY has a useful website. Their research concerning male victims of domestic abuse is particularly helpful and is based on academic and government research figures.

3   Australian Bureau of Statistics, *Personal Safety Survey Australia*, 2006.

internationally there is a greater need for recognition that males also suffer as victims of domestic abuse.

CHARITIES

One charity in the United Kingdom committed to helping male victims of domestic abuse is the *Mankind Initiative: Helping Men Escape from Domestic Abuse.* They claim to be the first U.K. charity 'to support male victims' and that they are 'at the forefront of providing services and support for male victims and campaigning for support'. The charity receives calls from male 'victims across all age ranges and professions', from 'dustmen and medical doctors to bankers and builders; from men in their twenties to men in their eighties and from men in England, Northern Ireland, Scotland and Wales'. The charity was registered in 2001. Another charity *PARITY* was formed in 1986 as the Campaign for Equal State Pension Ages but its brief has been widened to obtain equal rights for men and women on important issues. These two charities with others have been critical of public policy over nearly fifty years, a policy which has failed to support male victims. Further details concerning male victims of domestic abuse in England and Wales may help to highlight this aspect of the problem:

- Fathers who are victims of domestic abuse are vulnerable. If they report the abuse, they may be forced to leave home and possibly have little contact with the children. They are often unlikely to be given care of their children.
- If a father who suffers abuse leaves home with his children he can face a charge of abducting the children or child.
- There are several hundred funded refuges for women victims and their children to go to for safety. By contrast,

- only a handful of refuges are available for male victims of abuse and their children.
- Men account for one-third of all victims of abuse in intimate domestic relationships.
- Even fewer male victims report domestic abuse to the police.
- Those campaigning for male victims of domestic abuse claim that the men are often treated as 'second-class victims' and are not taken seriously by the police and social agencies.
- Similarly, in the United States of America, men represent about 40 per cent of victims experiencing severe physical violence domestically from an intimate partner.

SOME MALE VICTIMS

Here are recent examples of men being abused by their wives, with one being killed.

a) 'Horrendous abuse'

A British couple were married in Las Vegas even though there was 'horrendous' abuse of the solicitor husband, Dave Edwards. The father-of-one was stabbed by his wife Sharon, 42, in the chest with a kitchen knife in August 2015, only two months after they married. The police reported that the murder occurred 'after a culmination of months of abuse and violent outbursts'. The police spokesman, after the trial, revealed that the victim was 'embarrassed by the fact he was being abused by his wife, and seemed to just accept his situation, ignoring advice from friends to seek help'. Sharon Edwards was jailed for life with a minimum of twenty years.[4] The brother of the murdered victim said the death had highlighted the need for male victims of domestic abuse to 'speak out'. Outside the court,

---

4   *The Telegraph*, '"Bullying" bride given life for murdering solicitor husband was previously convicted of attacking ex-boyfriend' 9 March 2016.

the brother shared frankly, claiming men fear coming forward for it will be interpreted as a 'sign of weakness'. Frequently the victim arrived in work badly bruised after coffee tables and ash trays had been thrown at him but he had submitted to her demands in order to conceal her behaviour. Domestic abuse is 'not exclusive' to age, sex, status or profession. The Crown Prosecution Service affirmed there is a 'significant' under-reporting of domestic abuse against male victims; some of those reasons we have referred to.[5]

b) 'Unspoken abuse'

In England, victim Edward Charles[6] provides a detailed but chilling account of the horrific abuse he experienced. This is another heart-breaking story. Edward met his future wife, Augie, in a work situation and his first impressions of her were favourable. She appeared to be a 'settled person who loved her one-year-old son', though recently estranged from her husband. Although she confided in Edward and they gradually became close friends, he sensed she was not being open with him. Over many months of ups and downs, Edward began to feel that he loved her. Eventually they began living together. It was then that the physical violence commenced and as he was ironing the clothes one day, she grabbed the hot iron and pushed it across his wrist. On another occasion she stubbed her cigarette on his hand but then she would be normal in her behaviour for several months. Their baby daughter, Faith, was born in 2004 and Augie now became extremely critical of Edward, calling him a 'useless father' and the verbal abuse gathered momentum. She took control of

---

5   In 2016 in Caernarvon Crown Court, the judge allowed a woman abuser to walk free from the Court after she had battered her male partner around the head with a torch. That was only days after he had been treated in hospital for a heart attack.

6   Charles, E *The Unspoken Abuse: A Diary of Domestic Abuse*, (Great Britain: H&D Services, 2013), 2nd Edition.

their finances and continued her physical and verbal abuse as she manipulated the relationship for her own ends. Early in 2010 Edward suspected she was planning further harm as she became involved in another affair. In desperation he reported the abuse to the police and later to the social services and was 'shocked by their response'. A complicated sequence of events followed in which his wife weaved stories of deceit and malice to persuade the police, the social services and eventually the Family Court that Edward himself was the abuser rather than the victim. Edward expresses his disillusionment with the police as they 'tried their best to deflect the blame on to the victim'. He adds: 'While seeking truth and justice it is very hard to get anyone to listen'. In the light of recent action by the government to respond more sensitively and speedily to all victims of domestic abuse, one hopes that Edward's fight for justice is succeeding.[7] He has some final advice for readers who are in abusive relationships: *'Please take care and be safe. If you feel you are in an unsafe environment, then get out right away and report it. Don't do what I did and try to ignore the abuse otherwise it is already too late!'*

Men then are also victims of domestic abuse, and this fact must be recognised, though numerically more women suffer domestic abuse. In a later chapter, a former church pastor in the United Kingdom will relate his own experience of domestic abuse.

In the next chapter, we consider ways in which the term 'domestic abuse' is understood and defined. This is necessary in order to understand the complex nature of domestic abuse.

---

7   It is possible to follow Edward Charles's battle for justice on twitter at: @edwardcharles07 or visit his web page for regular updates as he seeks justice on behalf of himself but especially his daughter: *www.the unspokenabuse.com*

ACTION POINTS

1. Ought church leaders to do more in creating a greater awareness of domestic abuse? Give reasons for your answer.

2. Identify the difficulties facing male victims of domestic abuse in reporting their abuse?

4. Understanding Domestic Abuse: Continuing Challenges

What do the equivalent terms 'domestic abuse' and 'domestic violence' mean? There is no simple answer but The United Kingdom Government provides the following definition:

> *'any incident or patterns of incidents of controlling, coercive, threatening behaviour, violence or abuse between those aged 16 or over who are, or have been, intimate partners or family members regardless of gender or sexuality. The abuse can encompass but is not limited to psychological, physical, sexual, financial or emotional aspects.'*[1]

There can be difficulties interpreting and applying this definition. For example, ***'Controlling'*** behaviour involves a range of actions intended to make a person dependent and to isolate her/him from available support and resources. This may include preventing an individual from exercising independence and personal decision-making by planning their daily routine and blocking possible avenues of escape. There may be no physical violence yet the 'control' often reduces the victim to the level of a slave in the home. 'Controlling' behaviour is more frequently accompanied by ***'coercive'*** behaviour in the form of threats but also actions of assault intended to humiliate, frighten, harm and punish the victim. A 'milestone' legal case in May 2018 regarding coercive behaviour found

---

1   GOV.UK *Domestic Violence and Abuse* Home Office: Updated 27-3-2015.

Steven Saunders guilty of 'coercive and controlling behaviour' and he was sentenced to eighteen months imprisonment.[2] Soon after Saunders had met Ami, he began to change in his behaviour and treatment of her. He insisted on using her bank account and credit card, sold her mobile and controlled who she could talk to. When she talked of leaving, he threatened to harm himself and the emotional blackmail continued. They were eventually reduced to poverty and slept rough, despite her being pregnant. More examples will be given of controlling and coercive behaviour in later chapters but we emphasise here the fact that domestic abuse extends far beyond physical violence.

BULLYING

Referring again to the murder of solicitor Dave Edwards by his wife, Mr Justice William David told the abuser: 'You have a violent and bullying nature. This deadly attack with a deadly weapon was the culmination of long-term bullying by you...' Then there were also the wife's threats for her husband not to report her actions to anyone but to continue affirming that he loved her! The Senior Crown prosecutor regarded this case as 'another in the sad catalogue of violent repressive relationships that seem to rob the victim of their power or ability to stop the violence'. Such controlling and coercive behaviour by the abuser often enslaves the victim, whether women or men, in a web of cruelty and secrecy as well as fear. The British Government introduced a new law for England and Wales in 2015 which made 'controlling or coercive behaviour in intimate or familial relationships' a crime.

---

2   *Telegraph*, 'When she threatened to leave, he threatened to kill himself: the story behind a landmark coercive control case' 16 May 2018.

GUIDELINES

On behalf of the General Synod of the Church of England, a Working Group published *Responding to Domestic Abuse: Guidelines for those with pastoral responsibilities.*[3] Their working definition of domestic abuse is: 'Any incident of threatening behaviour, violence or abuse (**psychological, physical, sexual, financial or emotional**) between adults who are or have been intimate partners or family members, regardless of gender or sexuality'. This is similar to the later Government definition. The Working Group added that their definition is the 'Core Definition agreed by the Governmental Inter-Ministerial group on domestic violence'. While the General Synod referred to 'domestic violence' in 2004, this Group rightly preferred the term 'domestic abuse' in order to cover the range of abuse which occurs. Their explanation of terms used in explaining domestic abuse is extremely helpful. There is the reminder, for example, that on 'rare occasions' the abuse occurs only once but normally it is 'a systematic, repeated and often escalating pattern of behaviour…'[4] They do not claim to provide an exhaustive list of examples of abuse yet nevertheless their examples are valuable and instructive.

EXAMPLES

Under **physical** domestic abuse, the Report refers to:

hitting, slapping, burning, pushing, restraining, giving too much or the wrong medication, assault, kicking, biting, punching, shoving, smashing someone's possessions, imprisoning them or forcing them to use illegal drugs as a way of blackmail and control.

Examples given of **psychological** abuse are:

---

3   Church House Publishing, London, 2006.

4   *Responding to Domestic Abuse*, pp. 5-6.

shouting, swearing, frightening, blaming, ignoring or humiliating someone, blackmail, threatening harm to children or pets...ridiculing appearance and skills...obsessively and irrationally jealous, isolating them from friends and family, threatening suicide or self-harm.

One fears that 'shouting, frightening, blaming, ignoring or humiliating someone' can occur often within many homes– even Christian homes– as something which is tolerated as normal. Nevertheless, for Christians this is unbiblical behaviour to be repented of. Suggested examples of **financial** abuse include:

illegal or unauthorized use of someone's property, money, pension book or other valuables, forcing them to take out loans, keeping them in poverty then control of expenditure or use of transport or withholding money to pay for it.

For **sexual** abuse, details include

forcing someone to take part in any sexual activity without consent, e.g. rape or sexual assault; forcing them or blackmailing them into sexual acts with other people; forcing children to watch sexual acts; sexual name calling; imposition of dress codes upon a partner; involvement in the sex trade or pornography; knowingly passing on Sexually Transmitted Infections; controlling access to contraception.

RAPE

The specific criminalisation of marital rape in the United Kingdom has gathered momentum in recent decades so that legally marriage no longer gives license to rape one's own wife. Previously, under British common law, husbands were exempt from prosecution for raping their wives on the basis that marriage entailed consent to sex. However, in the early 1990s this exemption was abolished in response to a Law Commission report then a crucial 1991 House of Lords

ruling that husbands' immunity for rape within marriage no
longer formed part of English common law.[5] According to UN
reports, a growing number of countries have also amended
their legislation to make marital rape a criminal offence.
Sexual intercourse, therefore, within marriage needs to be
consensual rather than forced upon a partner against her or his
will. What is striking in the stories of clergy wives in Australia
who suffered domestic abuse was the prevalence of rape. Only
when some talked to friends did they recognise that they were
being raped illegally within marriage. Kylie, for example, was
tired of being treated by her clergy husband incessantly, night
and day, as a mere sex object. One morning when preparing to
leave the marital home permanently, her husband raped her
and in desperation she reported it to the police as a criminal
offence.[6]

SPIRITUAL ABUSE

Unlike many other definitions and examples of domestic abuse,
this Church of England Working Group also identifies the area
of **spiritual** abuse, providing telling and helpful examples like:

> *telling someone God hates them, refusing to let them worship...or go to
> church, using faith as a weapon to control and terrorise them for the
> abuser's personal pleasure or gain; using religious language to justify
> abuse (e.g. 'submit to your husband'), or to compel forgiveness.*

Once again, this type of abuse appears at times within
Christian marriages and this should be borne in mind in terms
of the church's teaching ministry. While it is hurtful for the
victim, the abuser often feels justified in quoting Scripture to

5   Https://www.opendemocracy.net/5050/sasha-hart/rape-marriage-and-rights,   14
     June 2014.

6   Some conservative websites encourage married men not to tolerate the wife's
     refusal of sex. Such a refusal is regarded by some as 'sinful rebellion against God's
     design'. See *Biblical Gender Roles.com (America)*.

sanction his behaviour. Later stories from victims will refer to this cruel aspect of abuse. Recent developments have given wider publicity to this aspect of abuse. For example, a Church of England Bishops' disciplinary tribunal decided that one of its clergy had been guilty of spiritual abuse while the Churches Children Pastoral Advisory Service (CCPAS) released a report on its on-line survey of churchgoers in which two-thirds felt they had personally experienced spiritual abuse. Questions are now being asked as to whether it is appropriate to use the term 'spiritual abuse' as a separate category of abuse rather than considering it as an abuse of power and an example of coercion. This will be discussed in a later chapter.

Under another sub-title of **'Neglect'** we are informed that this kind of abuse includes: *'depriving someone of food, shelter, heat, clothing, comfort, essential medication or access to medical care'*. Although aspects of these definitions may not be easily recognised by government or specialist agencies dealing with domestic abuse or in a Court of Law, they are helpful in pointing to the wide range of domestic abuse, in addition to physical violence. It is also helpful to see what may be involved in financial, psychological and spiritual abuse. On the other hand, some categories may be too detailed because a marriage partner may tend to shout, blame, threaten or humiliate their partner occasionally without intending to abuse. It may be interpreted as a temporary loss of temper or frustration within a secure, loving relationship rather than domestic abuse.

Another downside from a legal perspective is in proving the degree and regularity of abuse and whether or not the partner has been humiliated or deprived and 'controlled' abusively. Reflecting on domestic abuse, Claire Smith refers helpfully to 'a spectrum of behaviour'[7] with kicking, choking, beating and the use of weapons at the high end of the spectrum while

7   Smith, Claire, *God's Good Design*, (Australia: Matthias Media, 2012), p. 183.

further down the spectrum a greater degree of subjectivity enters into recognising coercion or threats. At what degree, for example, does intimidation in terms of a stare or gesture become threatening? For that reason, Smith talks of 'fuzzy edges' and warns against 'simple and neat definitions and categories'.

U.K. RESPONSES

In the 1970s and 1980s in the U.K., domestic abuse was generally regarded as a personal problem between a husband and wife and they were expected either to settle the problem or live with it. In fact, many folk assumed that the woman usually started the abuse or provoked the man to act violently towards her so she needed to mend her ways. If the police were called, they normally understood it to be only a domestic quarrel which the couple must resolve themselves. Rarely would they treat it as a criminal offence. It is not surprising therefore that Jenny Smith, herself a victim of domestic violence, could justifiably claim, *'so few people realise what life was like for battered wives as we were branded back then in 1970'*.[8] Because marriage was given considerable status in society, it was invariably agreed that the victim should remain within the marriage, no matter how violent the abuser was. And there was nowhere for the wife to go with her children[9]. That was Jenny Smith's experience – she was desperate with nowhere to go with her two small children. Her life was in danger with a husband becoming progressively more violent. One morning she called in at the local shop to buy milk and scanned the pages of a national newspaper when her eyes fastened on a

---

8   Smith, Jenny, *The Refuge: My Journey to the Safe House for Battered Women*, (London/ New York/Sydney/Toronto. New Delhi: Simon & Schuster, 2014), p. 292.

9   The British Office for National Statistics published in November 2017 show there were 274 refuge services offering support to victims of domestic abuse in England in 2017. This is 20 fewer than in 2012 but the number of available beds has risen in the period from 3,467 to 3,798.

small advert: *'Victim of domestic violence. Need help?'* She bought the newspaper and hid it under the carpet at home but only after cutting out the phone number in the advert. Another day she raced to the local shop where she was allowed to use their phone and call the number given in the advert. The call was answered immediately by a woman with a welcoming voice who gave her the address of a house used as a refuge by the Chiswick Women's Aid. With the help of a neighbour she ran out of her apartment with her two small children and eventually reached the Refuge in Chiswick.[10] 'I was so overcome ... the relief was utterly overwhelming... For the first time in years, I felt protected'.[11]

Jenny Smith describes the refuge as *'a women's shelter, a refuge, a sanctuary, a safe haven ... before Chiswick there had simply been nowhere for battered women to go, apart from the streets ... Chiswick gave these women a chance. It gave them a safe place to recover and plan their next move.'*[12] For Jenny Smith, she was able to rebuild her life and protect her children but many other victims remained in violent relationships.

SOCIAL PROBLEM

Today domestic abuse is recognised in the U.K. as a significant social problem. While serving in Government as Home Secretary, for example, Theresa May declared in March 2014: *'Domestic violence ruins lives and is completely unacceptable ... it has been one of my priorities.'*[13] She also took an initiative to improve police response to victims of domestic abuse after systematic

---

10   This refuge opened in 1971. This was the world's first women's refuge and it was the result of the vision and work of its founder, Erin Pizzey. There are now many such places in the U.K.. On any given day in 2017, this network supports more than 4,600 women and children with a tiny number of houses too for male victims of domestic abuse.

11   Smith, J, p. 173.

12   Smith, J, p. 178-179.

13   gov.uk. Announcement, 27 March 2014.

failings had been identified. Only months later, she announced the national roll-out of the Domestic Violence Disclosure Scheme (DVDS) – also known as Clare's Law – designed to provide victims with information that may protect them from an abusive situation before tragedy struck. Following a request, the police would be allowed to disclose information about a partner's previous history regarding domestic abuse or violent acts. This was followed by the Domestic Violence Protection Order (DVPO) enabling police and magistrates' courts to provide protection to victims in the immediate aftermath of a domestic abuse incident. As Prime Minister, Theresa May launched a major consultation to research a domestic abuse law with new measures to help victims in an attempt 'to transform the way the U.K. thought about tackling domestic abuse'.[14] The Prime Minister describes government action as representing a 'tough new approach' which will better protect victims by enabling courts to impose a range of conditions on abusers. There could be 'compulsory alcohol treatment, attending a programme to address their underlying attitudes or addictions, and using electronic tagging to monitor them'. It is also hoped to appoint a Domestic Abuse Commissioner to hold the government to account. Economic abuse will be recognised for[15] the first time'. Those working to address this problem welcome the Consultation and the government's intention to confer then introduce new measures. For example, the Chief Executive of *Women's Aid*, Katie Ghose, is 'delighted' and wants 'to ensure that every survivor and her child can safely escape domestic abuse'. In supporting the government's action, Suzanne Jacob who directs the domestic abuse charity *SafeLives* adds that 'the time for piecemeal sticking plasters

---

14 *The Guardian*, 'New measures on violence against women to be put in domestic abuse bill', 17 February 2018.

15 *Https://www.uk/government-takes-action-to-tackle-domestic-abuse-GOV.UK*

is over, we need radical change, and we will stand side-by-side with survivors to make this happen'. Similarly, the charity *Refuge* 'applauds the intentions of the government to put survivors at the heart of its efforts to stamp out domestic abuse'. Mark Brooks who chairs the *ManKind Initiative* charity, has called for a 'real step change' too from the government in supporting and recognising male victims of domestic violence which represent approximately one-third of all victims.[16]

MURMURINGS

There were murmurings, however, from the police for they appeared to be criticised for failing to respond vigorously enough to the problem. For example, Nigel McCrery served with the Nottinghamshire Constabulary, a city known for its domestic abuse. He reports that in his experience the majority of abusers were men. McCrery describes some of his experiences dealing with domestic abuse:

> *I have seen women with broken noses, black eyes and teeth smashed. I've seen pregnant women kicked in the stomach by men so brutal it defies understanding … I have also seen a woman without a single injury, trembling with fear. She admitted her partner had never touched her, he didn't need to because he ruled her by terror, destroying her confidence and making her feel she was worthless.*

After arresting the abuser and taking statements from witnesses, at least half of the victims would visit the police station the next day or soon afterwards on their own or with the abuser in order to withdraw the complaint. The police were then unable to take further action in those situations.[17]

---

16   See in addition: http://www.bbc.co.uk/news/uk-3901124
17   *The Spectator*, 19 May 2016.

IMPROVEMENT

With the government consultation under way in 2018, it is important to acknowledge a marked improvement in police response and understanding of domestic abuse yet:

- There are on average thirty-five domestic assaults on a woman before the victim calls the police.
- Less than 50 per cent of all domestic abuse incidents are reported to the police.
- The police receive one domestic abuse call every minute of the day.
- Police body cameras now make it easier to prosecute. While there were just over 70,700 prosecutions in 2012/2013, the figure has risen to just under 100,000 by 2016.

A more novel programme was introduced by the regional government in **Scotland** to tackle domestic abuse. The programme, AVDR – **A**sk, **V**alidate, **D**ocument and **R**efer – is a Scottish backed -programme training hairdressers, firefighters, veterinary surgeons, medical doctors and teachers to recognise signs of domestic abuse and to raise it in conversations with individuals in routine appointments and contact time.

ELDERLY

Another aspect of domestic abuse relates to elderly people. One example is the warning which the Older People's Commissioner for Wales provided. Here is an independent voice alerting society to ways in which the elderly can suffer domestic abuse. The Commissioner removes the myth that domestic abuse is something which only affects younger couples; '*rather anyone can be a victim of domestic abuse and sexual violence*'. In fact, the harsh reality is that, '*for some older people, it will have been a significant feature for most of their adult lives, an on-going problem for 20, 30 and 40 years or even longer.'*

One woman in the United Kingdom, a victim of domestic abuse, recently reported to me:

> *I work with older people, and am commonly advising women, many of whom are in their 70s, 80s and 90s, to leave their abusive husbands. Often the men are my patients, they develop dementia, and the verbal and physical abuse within marriage worsens (I say worsens, the women tell me that their husbands have always been bullies)… I have had 4 instances of severe domestic abuse in the last few months. However, none of the women ended up leaving their violent husbands.[18]*

However, for some the abuse will commence only when they reach an older age and/or become frail or cognitively impaired. It is estimated that over 40,000 older people in Wales are being abused in their own homes every year regardless of their gender, ethnic background, sexual orientation or gender identity. Regretfully, those with a disability are at greater risk of being abused. The abuser can be a spouse, ex-spouse/partner, son, son-in-law, daughter, daughter-in-law, grandchild or a member of the extended family but sometimes there may be multiple abusers.[19] This same report also refers to physical, sexual, psychological/emotional and financial abuse with coercive control as being the main areas of domestic abuse. Under financial abuse, the Older People's Commissioner for Wales includes *'stealing money or possessions, being made to give money, possessions or property. The use of fraud to take money, possessions or property. Taken or kept power of attorney or attempt to take or keep power of attorney'.*

---

18   Email correspondence October 2017.

19   *Domestic abuse and sexual violence: help and Support for Older People in Wales,* Older People's Commissioner for Wales, Cardiff, undated.

One fears that such financial abuse and coercive control of the elderly is more widespread than is reported and, in many cases, the offences committed are 'criminal'. The abuse of older people 'is a hidden, and often ignored, problem in society ... it is impossible to quantify how many older people are being abused at any one given time'.[20] Elderly abuse occurs within their own home, a carer's home, day care, residential care, a nursing home or in hospital.

SUMMARY

The Crime Survey of England and Wales (CSEW) estimate that 1.3 million women experienced domestic abuse in the year ending March 2016 with possibly as many as 4.3 million women having experienced domestic abuse at some point in their lives from the age of sixteen. A word of caution is provided by agencies like Women's Aid that domestic abuse is *'very common, however, and this is often difficult to quantify'*. It is *'a largely hidden crime'*. The Welsh Women's Aid provide a more comprehensive and annual estimate of the problem of abuse: *'It is estimated that around three million women across the U.K. experience rape, domestic violence, forced marriage, stalking, sexual exploitation, trafficking and other forms of violence every year. This is equivalent to the population of Wales.'*

USA: DEFINITION AND FACTS

How is domestic abuse understood in America? The United States Department of Justice defines domestic abuse/violence as:

a pattern of abusive behaviour in any relationship that is used by one partner to gain or maintain power and control over another intimate partner. Domestic violence can be physical, sexual, emotional, economic

---

20   *Responding to domestic abuse: Guidelines,* London, Church Publishing House, 2006, pp. 40-43.

or psychological actions or threats … including any behaviours that intimidate, manipulate, humiliate, isolate, frighten, terrorize, coerce, threaten, blame, hurt, injure or wound someone.

A further explanation is given concerning emotional and economic abuse:

Emotional *abuse involves 'undermining an individual's sense of self-worth and/or self-esteem' which may include, 'but is not confined to constant criticism, diminishing one's abilities, name-calling or damaging one's relationship with his/her children.'*

Economic *abuse involves making a person 'economically/financially dependent by total control over financial resources, withholding access to money or forbidding attendance at school/college or employment'.*

In America, domestic abuse is a major social problem. The National Coalition Against Domestic Violence (NCADV) reports that on average nearly twenty people per minute are physically abused by an intimate partner, equivalent to more than ten million men and women annually. Nearly three women are killed daily by an intimate partner while one in three women and one in four men have been victims of some form of domestic abuse by an intimate partner in their life-time. One well-known example in America has been the abusive relationship and consequent separation of Johnny Depp, the star in the *Pirates of the Caribbean* films and the actress Amber Heard. Only married for fifteen months by the summer of 2016, the actress explained:

I endured excessive emotional, verbal and physical abuse from Johnny, which has included angry, hostile, humiliating and threatening assaults to me whenever I questioned his authority or disagreed with him … Johnny's paranoia, delusions and aggression increased throughout our relationship … I am extremely afraid of Johnny and for my safety. I am petrified he will return at any moment.

Once again, the main features of domestic abuse surfaced in this strained relationship as physical violence was accompanied by emotional, verbal and psychological abuse.

MORE FACTS

In the United States of America, while one third of all women in the United States experience domestic violence, approximately 40 per cent of the victims of severe physical and psychological abuse were men. New York City Police Department respond to about 280,000 domestic incidents of abuse annually[21]. In America, the National Coalition Against Domestic Violence (NCHDV) report the following facts:

- On average, nearly twenty people per minute are physically abused by an intimate partner. In one year, this is equivalent to over ten million men and women!
- On average, more than 20,000 phone calls are received by domestic abuse/violence hotlines nationwide.
- The National Domestic Violence Hotline includes stalking and rape within its domestic abuse/violence statistics, providing a figure of over twelve million men and women annually who suffer such abuse.
- Nearly three women in the United States are killed daily by an intimate partner.
- Seven million children live in families where severe domestic violence occurs with a traumatic impact on their lives.
- The National Domestic Violence Hotline report that twenty-four people per minute in America are victims of rape, physical violence or stalking by an intimate

---

21   New York City Mayor's Office: To Combat Domestic Violence: Fact Sheet, 2015.

partner, amounting to over twelve million men/women a year.

Against this background, the plight of children who witness various forms of domestic abuse in families will be highlighted later in chapter nine.

In the next chapters we will narrow the focus further by considering domestic abuse in some Christian families. A number of Christian victims will describe their experience of abuse, some for the very first time. They need to be listened to.

ACTION POINTS

1. Reflect on the various aspects of domestic abuse referred to in this chapter.

2. Are there additional responses you would like to see with regard to addressing the problem of domestic abuse?

3. In which additional ways can you and your church care for the elderly? Share your suggestions with others with a view to positive action.

PART 2
DOMESTIC ABUSE IN CHRISTIAN FAMILIES: VICTIMS SPEAK OUT

5. Victims Begin to Tell Their Story

An important book published in 1989 shocked Christians and churches in America and in the United Kingdom. It was a disturbing read. Was it true? Could these things happen today in Bible teaching churches and Christian homes? Was this something occurring in my church and in the homes of any of my Christian friends? These were questions raised by readers of the book. I am referring to *Battered into Submission: The Tragedy of Wife Abuse in the Christian Home.*[1] The authors of this book, James and Phyllis Alsdurf, were themselves shocked some eight years earlier when they were confronted with the phenomenon unexpectedly.

'STUNNED'

When Phyllis Alsdurf was editor of the magazine *Family Life Today*, she wrote about the abuse of wives in Christian homes. She had listened to the stories of several Christian women who had the courage to relate their experiences. The author was 'stunned' by the existence and extent of the problem in Christian families but just as shocked to discover who the abusers were, including pastors, respected Christian businessmen and other active church members. They talked about God's love while living a lie. Normally, no one in their

---

1   Alsdurf, James and Phyllis, *Battered into Submission: The Tragedy of Wife Abuse in the Christian Home* (Illinois: InterVarsity Press, 1989).

churches knew what was happening in these homes and battered wives were too afraid to report it. Would they be believed anyway if they reported it? Just as important was the question who could they trust? Also, would that individual keep the information confidential? Phyllis and her husband felt strongly that they ought to research the problem further and they were encouraged by others to do so and pursued the subject for approximately eight years. Phyllis and James Alsdurf were concerned that underlying attitudes to abuse were hardly changing, even in churches. They felt 'outrage' that such behaviour occurred and persisted in some Christian homes.

SIGNIFICANT

The book is significant in at least three ways. For example, it was a pioneer in confronting churches regarding the extent of domestic abuse in some Christian homes. The book also touched on various aspects of the problem, such as why an abused wife chooses to stay in an abusive relationship, the kind of men who abuse their wives, and crucial subjects like marriage and divorce and challenging traditional pastoral responses. The book highlighted the poor response of church leaders and the lack of understanding concerning the problem. Often these women were advised by church leaders to stay with an abusive husband or they would be criticised or even rejected for not doing so, however violent the abuser was. Nevertheless, the book's impact was limited and domestic abuse continues unabated in churches. In the following chapters we are providing a sample of authentic stories of domestic abuse in Christian families. The victims are eager for you to know how they suffered but not in order to draw attention to themselves. Rather they really want to help other victims and also encourage church leaders to pastor lovingly and wisely those experiencing abuse. Listen to their stories.

EXAMPLE 1: MARY, BRIAN AND ANN

The family belonged to a small pastorless church in a South Wales valley town and were faithful in attendance. The husband had occasionally preached there while the children in the morning service regularly recited Bible verses they had memorised. One Sunday a regular visiting preacher noticed that the family was absent. The preacher assumed the children were ill so decided to visit them after the morning service. As he rang the doorbell, he heard shouting from inside the house then a seven-year-old girl and nine-year-old boy opened the door. They were relieved to see him and invited him inside. The children were upset while Mary, the mother, appeared tense, her face pale and her hair ruffled; there was embarrassment as she tried to cover up what had happened. Unknown to the preacher – then or since – when he rang the doorbell, the husband was strangling her. Screaming, the children struggled to defend her, but their father persistently kicked them away. Only a few more seconds and their mother would have died. That pastoral visit saved her life. The husband fled via the rear door on hearing the doorbell. Despite the couple's church involvement, no one knew the ugly secrets of their family life. The abuse was physical on that and other occasions, but it had also been psychological and manipulative; the children feared their father and his moods. I knew the family well and although living at a distance from them my wife and I soon became involved pastorally. There was a need to listen to, and care for, this vulnerable family; the incident was the culmination of a long process of fear, mood swings, violence, lies and abuse. The wife had kept secret much of what happened over the years, despite her parents' suspicions. The children were profoundly affected by the abuse and they will be referred to in chapter nine. Although I met with the husband a few times afterwards, there was no happy ending, for his wife and children needed protection from him. This led eventually to divorce but only after the wife had wrestled with the question. For Christians embroiled in domestic abuse this is a major issue and there is confusion concerning the biblical principles regarding divorce.

EXAMPLE 2: LUCILLE AND ROBERT

This example is taken from James and Phyllis Alsdurf's book *Battered into Submission* because I am reminding you that domestic abuse is not an exclusively British problem. This example further underlines the fact that domestic abuse exists within some Christian families. Sometimes the husband may have a prominent church position like pastor or a church officer and be widely respected. And we should not be shocked to learn that victims of abuse, even Christians, can be so desperate and provoked that they may retaliate in self-defence. While their motive may be self-defence and the desire to stop the abuse at least temporarily they may actually hurt or even kill the abuser. It can happen in a Christian home! Only a few victims resort to force as a means of self-defence yet almost all victims of domestic abuse feel the same sense of desperation and despair. This fact needs to be appreciated. This example follows a similar pattern to others we have given. Within ten months of Lucille marrying Robert, the abuse started by the husband hitting her hard repeatedly and, on several occasions, despite her pregnancy. Lucille quickly identified a pattern in the abuse. It was when the husband perceived that she was disobeying him and flouting his authority that he became violent. While Lucille was entirely submissive to her husband, it was impossible to please him. He 'expected perfection from us', she explains.[2] The children were also included in the physical beatings, including their seven-year old son who was suffering from the effects of a stroke. When the son died and Lucille went into the bedroom to cry, the husband beat her again and later too on returning from the funeral. Common to other experiences of domestic abuse, psychological, financial, emotional and spiritual abuse accompanied the physical violence. His behaviour was 'coercive' and 'controlling' by means of threats, humiliating words and behaviour towards her with the purpose of isolating her and regulating her daily schedule. Her husband lived a double life. He was a pastor but also director of a Christian school. Then his inappropriate relationship with a young teenage girl leaked out and over those days he was particularly cruel in beating Lucille and their children. He announced he intended to kill her after he had rested and knowing that he always carried out his threats, Lucille froze with fear, but too afraid to tell anyone, she took her husband's gun and shot him. Eventually she was acquitted of murder on the ground of her husband's abusive behaviour towards her and the children. The inevitable question arises again. Why did Lucille and the children fail to report the situation to the police and social agencies? The answer is complex. Certainly, fear was a major factor deterring them from reporting the abuse. The fear factor was reinforced by threats of punishment if they exposed the abuser. 'I was scared of leaving', Lucille explained, 'because he had threatened that if I ever left he would come and find me and the boys, and all that would be left would be pieces.' She knew he meant it so she was protecting her children as well as herself. There was also the way in which she and the children had been made completely dependent on husband Robert. There was a distortion of biblical teaching on the abuser's part. The words

2   Alsdurf, pp. 14-16.

of Scripture the husband highlighted but misinterpreted were Ephesians 5, verses 22-24: *'wives, submit to your own husbands, as to the Lord … so let the wives be* [subject] *to their own husbands in everything'*. We will consider this question further in chapter twelve. Strangely, despite all the abuse suffered in the home, Lucille and the children still loved the man who abused them. Some may find this difficult to understand but the complex mixture of fear, desperation and love often co-exist in abusive relationships so this becomes another factor making them reluctant to expose their husband/father abuser.

EXAMPLE 3: GRAHAM AND EDITH

Despite many similarities between cases of domestic abuse, there are also differences – sometimes major differences. This fourth example contrasts with those I have already given for there was no psychological abuse or coercive behaviour; no threats were made either. The major problem was alcohol. Several times a week Graham returned home drunk, either from work or after a night out. On these occasions he could be violent towards his wife. The bruises on her were often visible but she refused to report her husband or share details of the abuse with others. The reason for this refusal was not fear but a deep love and concern for her husband. When he was not drinking, he was a caring, supportive father/husband and a delight to be with. Graham was not a Christian though his wife, Edith, had come to faith in rather unexpected circumstances and with Graham's hearty approval! Spending time pastorally with the man was important. I liked him. He had high principles and loved his wife deeply and their children. Slowly he began to share his feelings. For Graham, alcohol was an escape mechanism in an attempt to cope with a deep-seated guilt complex. For years he had hated himself for what he had done, including his treatment of the wife he loved.

It was difficult living with himself but alcohol was addictive, a proven, attractive option which blotted out his guilt feelings for a few hours yet he hated what he did to his wife. He shared his problem with me. In World War II he was a young sailor serving in a Royal Navy submarine. One incident stood out for him. He was responsible for releasing a torpedo after his officer issued the command. On this particular day, the torpedo he released sank a German ship and he saw many people from the ship struggling and drowning in the sea. The images of those people drowning as the ship sank, stayed with him day and night. The flashbacks were vivid. His conscience accused him of killing the people. It was unbearable. Was there forgiveness? He doubted it and for a long period, he despaired of obtaining divine forgiveness. When he eventually conceded that God in Christ could forgive him, he felt encouraged. There was a problem, however. He was unable to forgive himself. Did he receive grace and forgiveness before dying? I do not know. But all abusers, including Graham, need to hear of God's rich and free grace super-abounding to undeserving sinners. Pastoral support in this situation involved making oneself available when he was ready to talk, encouraging and supporting his wife in different ways. This example of domestic abuse was alcohol related, a common cause of domestic abuse in many households and also in many countries. Not all abusers love their wives like Graham did and they may not have partners who remain in the situation and suffer ongoing violence. For Edith there were many days when she felt distressed and fearful of what may happen and she readily confessed that under such stress her reactions were sometimes far from exemplary.

4: MULTIPLE EXAMPLES – AUSTRALIA

The Anglican church in Australia is under close scrutiny by the news media[3] due to a significant number of clergy wives who claim they have suffered domestic abuse – yes, with their clergy husbands as the abusers! And it is uncomfortable reading. In the Autumn of 2017 a formal apology to all victims of domestic abuse in Anglican churches was led by Canon Grant at the Sydney Synod. He explained:

> *I, as a conservative, have not done enough to guard against the twistings of Scripture in ways that give comfort to abusers or that victims might hear as inviting them to continue as victims and not to get the help they need.*

For some victims like Jane, 'It means nothing because when I left I was treated like a criminal …. They wanted to get rid of me, wanted to pretend none of my abuse happened. There was no real support …. I need help and understanding…'. By contrast, Rebecca was pleased to have some acknowledgement but emphasised that 'an apology without action is empty.'

ONLINE SUPPORT GROUP

A private online support group of Anglican clergy wives abused by their husbands has emerged in New South Wales with the intention of encouraging and supporting each other. These wives were shocked at the number of clergy wives suffering such abuse and how common the problem appeared to be. Their experiences were also similar in that they had supported their husbands' ministry yet felt compelled to leave the marital relationship after years of emotional, physical, financial and sexual abuse. As a consequence, they suffered depression, fear and panic attacks with some grappling with suicidal thoughts.

---

3   *7.30 and ABC NEWS Australia:* 'Raped, tracked, humiliated: Clergy Wives speak out about domestic violence', Julia Baird and Hayley Gleeson.

VIOLENCE: JANE

Jane is a member of the online support group of Anglican clergy wives in New South Wales. Living in Sydney now as a single parent, she shared her story with *ABC NEWS*. Violent is the word she uses to describe her husband's treatment of her – a man who has been a senior Anglican priest working in parishes across Australia. 'He was sexually abusive from the start,' she explained. He enjoyed pornography, drank heavily and every night during their twenty-year marriage woke her up several times for sex until as a young mother she became sleep deprived and exhausted. Devastated, depressed and experiencing a breakdown, she eventually left her husband. Her faith remained strong despite suffering in so many ways.

FRUSTRATION

Early in 2017 an investigation by *7.30* and *ABC NEWS* discovered hundreds of women in Christian churches suffering domestic abuse, some of whom were wives of clergy from different denominations across Australia. Out of sheer frustration these wives contacted the media to share their stories and frustration that church leaders had failed to respond and to listen to them. What adds to the frustration of those within the Anglican denomination, is that church leaders have known about the existence of domestic abuse by clergy for several decades. The following details only add fuel to their frustrations.

DAMAGING EVIDENCE

There are important Archives belonging to the Centre Against Sexual Assault (CASA), part of the Royal Women's Hospital in Melbourne; these Archives include extensive details of research regarding violence in churches. The Archives identify two important dates illustrating the failure of the church to respond to the problem: **1990** marked CASA's first publication: *Pastoral Support to Churches on Sexual Violence Against Women and Children in the Church Community.* This was produced by CASA in collaboration with Anglican and Roman Catholic Churches, the Churches of Christ, the Uniting Church and the Salvation Army. This research established at least two important facts:

- that some clergymen were abusing their wives which included extensive sexual assaults.
- it was recommended that bishops and other church leaders should take urgent action.

A second important date was **1994,** the year CASA published their *Public Face. Private Pain: The Anglican Report About Violence Against Women and the Abuse of Power within the Church Community.*

Among the facts included in this publication were the following:

- Some wives were suffering physical and emotional abuse 'in silence'.
- 9 per cent of those interviewed were abused by male clergy.
- More than half of the victims had experienced sexual violence – significantly higher than other forms of abuse.
- Wives complained unanimously that it was more difficult to report abuse when the abuser was an ordained minister/clergyman.
- These wives were extremely distressed and disillusioned over the response of church leaders to their complaints of abuse by their clergy husbands.
- Wives were worried about the 'public image of the men' so they chose often to remain silent rather than risk criticism and rejection by the congregation and church leaders. Many women reported they had been

stigmatised when they eventually disclosed the abuse to church leaders.

- Rather than refer to domestic abuse incidents as 'marriage breakdown' or 'relationship difficulties', church leaders must understand the incidents as criminal behaviour.

- The researchers strongly condemned the practice of moving offenders to other parishes or roles such as chaplains or youth ministers. Their reasoning is that 'they are representatives of God's love, which is about trust, service, healing, leadership and respect for the vulnerable. Sexual violence ... should have serious and long-term consequences regarding their status as a priest.'

What is shocking, according to clergy wives interviewed by *ABC News*, is that very little had changed in the church since 1994.

PROGRESS?

On the other hand, in a different diocese – Tasmania – Bishop Richard Condie claims that if a complaint was received, 'the clergy person against whom the allegations were made would be immediately stood down.' In addition to the police being involved, a diocesan tribunal would also be convened. Similarly, in the Anglican diocese of Adelaide, Assistant Bishop Tim Harris insists that 'we now apply rigorous psychological testing before accepting (candidates) ... declined at least half-a-dozen candidates for concerns over inappropriate behaviour or character trends'. The problem is by no means confined to the Anglican Church in Australia. A spokeswoman for the Safe Churches Unit explains that her Unit, on behalf of the New South Wales Presbyterian Church, serves as a domestic violence overseer regarding ministers and church leaders. This has been 'on a small number of occasions in recent years'. Concerning Baptist churches in New South Wales, they can recall less than five allegations concerning domestic abuse by clergy. Each allegation is investigated 'extensively' and when necessary an independent investigator is used then appropriate disciplinary action is taken, if the allegation is substantiated.

AFTER ABUSE – WHAT?

For the wives who eventually leave their abusive clergy husbands, life can be very difficult and lonely. They also become homeless when leaving their husband as they live in a house provided by the church. There is often rejection of the wife by a church congregation for leaving her husband, probably a man they admire. For many of the victims, congregations are rarely informed of the real facts concerning the personal and domestic life of their spiritual leader. In the absence of a formal and reliable statement from the hierarchy, people form their own ideas as to the cause of the marital breakdown. In practice, this deprives the victim of potential support from the congregation in terms of prayer and practical help while, argues Isabella, it often allows the abuser to escape with his reputation untarnished. Poverty confronts many of these wives and if dependent children are involved then it is more difficult for the wife to cope.

SUPPORTIVE

Jane, in deciding to leave her abusive clergy husband after twenty years of marriage, felt that she faced a dark future. She trusted the Lord and believed in his providential care but the fears, doubts and practical needs were so real at times and overwhelming. At her lowest point, she was encouraged by a sympathetic Anglican minister who, she claims, 'saved her life.' One pastor and his wife', she says, 'was so instrumental in me leaving ... they were so supportive ... they helped me pack, move, and gave me food, meals and assured me, "We believe you."' That meant a great deal to her. Despite that encouragement and reminder of the Lord's provision, Jane has known times of discouragement as well as suffering panic attacks in going to church services, especially in the early months after separation. Another victim, **Emily,** says she is rediscovering her faith after being broken and battered by her abusive clergy husband for years. These wives are finding it is a slow process of rebuilding one's life and home as a single parent.

HELPFUL

The Australian examples are helpful in understanding more about domestic abuse in a Christian marriage. An earlier chapter highlighted fear as a prominent experience of victims and that is true in Australia. This fear, often emerging early on in marriage, develops over years as the wife becomes increasingly subject to threats, violence and bullying. In most cases, the pattern of abuse is predictable with the wife knowing that the abuser can react suddenly and cruelly at any moment and for irrational reasons. Such fear experienced over several years must not be underestimated. What appears strongly in the Australian examples is sexual violence in which the woman is regarded more as an object by the husband to relieve physical cravings rather than a person to be loved and cherished. Sexual intercourse does not occur on the basis of mutual consent but in the context of violence, disrespect and a dismissal of the wife's feelings or wishes. In Australia this is referred to as rape or sexual abuse. The Australian examples of domestic abuse are also useful in drawing further attention to the spiritual abuse which occurs when Scripture is misused in marriage. This point is fundamental and will be addressed in a later chapter. The stories of Rita and Louise, and their experience of domestic abuse will be shared in the next chapter. Both are strong Christians who live in the United Kingdom.

ACTION POINTS

1. Are you surprised, even 'stunned', by the existence of domestic abuse in some Christian marriages? Explain your answer.

2. From the examples provided in this chapter, identify ways in which pastoral care could be exercised or improved.

6. Victims: Rita and Louise

These two ladies, unknown to one another, are relating their experiences for the first time. Their circumstances and the extent of the abuse they suffered vary yet nevertheless both suffered domestic abuse. And both women thought they were marrying Christians and looked forward to serving and honouring the Lord in their marriages. For both women, the Lord's grace has sustained them, yet the consequences of abuse continue to affect them.

RITA

For Rita,[1] her experience of domestic abuse has spanned twenty years. A Christian, Rita thought that the young man from her church who proposed marriage to her was a godly believer and that they could serve the Lord together. He gave evidence of trusting Christ and was eager to share the gospel with other people, even preaching in churches. Very early in the marriage, however, there was a rude awakening for he began to be violent towards her but at the same time the psychological, emotional and spiritual abuse developed which was more difficult for her to cope with. A further aspect in her marital situation was her husband's addiction to pornography. In the early years it was by means of videos mailed to their

---

1   All the names of individuals referred to in this and other chapters are changed to ensure anonymity.

home; these were 'dirty' and she tried sometimes to render the videos useless. But the addiction continued and eventually developed into online pornography which was more secretive and extensive. She acknowledges that psychological abuse has had a 'massive impact' on her.

Her husband played mind games in twisting facts, even Bible verses, accusing her of being incompetent. Daily he told her she was 'ugly' and 'stupid', 'good for nothing', 'no one loves you', 'you are a rubbish wife' and 'a rubbish mother'. There was not a single day without verbal and psychological abuse or physical abuse – often violently, sometimes using objects like a knife. On the other hand, he continued preaching in churches, and maintained his public image in churches as a keen Christian worker. His public image contrasted sharply with his private and family life, even in front of his young children. No one outside knew there were problems, although a handful of close Christian friends had their suspicions. This relentless physical and psychological abuse led her partly to believe what he said about her. Rita felt numb and seemed to have no emotion; she felt 'crushed', 'scared', 'bullied' and 'isolated' as the abuse gathered momentum. She felt too ashamed to tell anyone.

There was also the fear that people would not believe her story. Another fear was that the abuse would increase if her husband discovered she had shared the secret with others. Coupled with this was the husband's threat to take the children from her if she reported the abuse. The 'bullying worked very well in keeping me quiet' she explains. Rita felt 'desperate' and she was 'bitterly disappointed' for her marriage was not what she imagined it would be like and instead of loving, her husband was critical, unkind and cruel. The marriage was a 'sham'; it was a 'hard slog' to keep going; more than once she thought, 'I have made a big mistake'. She felt locked in the secret world of domestic abuse and there seemed no way for her and the children to escape.

NEW DEVELOPMENTS

A new development in her situation was unexpected and independent of her entirely. Her husband was involved in a sad external situation of his own making which had major consequences for him. Independently again, the police learned of Rita's domestic abuse situation and help became available. The police's own Women's Safety Unit offered counselling and exercised a supportive role in varying degrees for about eight years until a Court Order was in place. It was only in this period she recognised that what she experienced was actually domestic abuse. The Women's Safety Unit also involved Women's Aid who arranged for their representative to visit her, but even more, Women's Aid kept in touch with her, changed the door/window locks as her estranged husband kept calling when she was out and removed things from the house. They also offered a 'Freedom' course; their help was invaluable.

TWISTS AND TURNS

Even throughout this period, it was difficult for Rita to think rationally and there was a continuing fear she might lose custody of her children. Suicidal thoughts had become stronger during the years; she was feeling 'desperate'. 'Despair' is another word Rita uses to describe her feelings. Bitterly disappointed with all her high expectations of marriage, she faced the harsh fact that her hopes and ideals were in ruins. In the mornings as time went on, she would 'wake up in a sweat and panic'. Following an extremely difficult and bitter separation then divorce, there were many court proceedings in which she gained the protection of the Court and custody of her children. These proceedings were unpleasant as her former husband contested her evidence but also defied the Court Orders, making life as difficult as possible for Rita. Government measures in reducing financial assistance meant it became too expensive for Rita to go to Court, even when it was necessary. While currently the contact with her abuser is minimal, the psychological and spiritual abuse continues by manipulating arrangements for his access to the children. The saga is ongoing but she is on the road to recovery. It has been a long road involving twists and turns as well as struggles and Rita will have suggestions to offer later to churches as to how they can help people like her come through the abuse and recover from the scars. Rita has proved the Lord in so many ways through years of abuse, pain and tears. She has also been able to encourage other women in similar situations by leading informal Bible studies in her home. I have observed over several years how the Word of God has become more and more precious to her. Despite all the abuse suffered, and so many hardships, the Lord has sustained her in his grace. Now she is entering a more encouraging period.

Key words used by Rita include:

'massive impact', 'violent', 'fear', 'ashamed', 'bullying', 'desperate', 'bitterly disappointed', 'sham', 'hard slog', 'despair', 'sweat and panic' and 'manipulating'.

LOUISE

I am delighted that Louise is sharing her own recent experience of domestic abuse. Her story illustrates the controlling and psychological aspects of domestic abuse with the consequent suffering and fear on her part.

Q: Tell us please, Louise, about your background.

A: *I grew up in a Christian home, became a Christian in my teens and went to University then later I married a man I thought was a Christian.*

Q: Did you know your husband well before marrying him?

A: *I thought I did! We married after courting for less than a year, but I had known him in University. It seemed quite quick, but I think it was due to a combination of things. Probably I married quickly as my husband wanted to make sure I didn't leave him. However, I was happy with that.*

Q: Was your husband a Christian?

A: *He would profess to be but I really don't think he is a Christian. He grew up in a non-Christian family, but always had Christian friends at school. At University he tended to gravitate towards Christians and lived in a house with some Christian girls. He liked Christian girls, as he thought they were kind and sweet, didn't get drunk or wear much make up! He was very popular when I met him first, lots of girls on my degree course liked him. We went out for a few weeks but split up as he cheated on me. I was not wise. I went out with him knowing he wasn't a Christian.*

Q: Why did you marry him then?

A: *He was courting someone else for a period and they split up. Not long after this he contacted me, said that he had become a Christian so we started going out and we married within the year. Several friends advised me not to marry him, citing that he could be moody (they had shared a house with him at university), and that I was a more mature Christian. My mum told me shortly before our wedding that she did not want me to marry him as we were a bad match. I knew she was right but did not feel I could pull out at that point. It felt so cruel.*

Initially we would pray and read the Bible together, but this did not continue once we were married. I think he professed faith so I would marry him.

Q: In the light of your experience, have you any advice to give to courting couples?

A: *I would advise dating couples to take things slowly. Date in the context of community. Socialise with your church family together. Listen to what other more mature Christians tell you. Spend time with older Christians, observe what is good in their marriages, or friendships. My sister split up with one boyfriend after having Sunday lunch with an older couple and observing how kind they were to each other. It made her realise that her boyfriend was not kind or thoughtful and that those things are important to her. She is glad that later she married a kind, godly man.*

Q: How was the relationship early in marriage?

A: *Things were good initially. I was happy. I did wonder whether I should have married someone different, in that I didn't feel we had much in common, but we seemed to get on ok.*

Q: What happened then?

A: *Within a year, things began to change. We had a baby and I became unhappy in my marriage. On reflection (and I did not see this until deciding to leave my husband) my relationship was a controlling one. We moved closer to my parents. My husband had previously got on with them, but the relationship changed. He stopped speaking with them and was very critical of them behind their backs. He was simply quite rude towards them. I did try to address this, but he accused me of siding with them and not being loyal to him. It seemed he wanted to isolate his small family of me, him and his daughter away from everyone else. He did not stop me from seeing my parents or siblings,* but he would behave so rudely to them that it made me not want to see them when he was going to be there.

Q: Was he violent?

A: *He started shouting at me and becoming angry quite easily. He never hit me but would often throw things at me. Once when he was angry he threw the baby bath against the wall above my head, breaking the bath.*

Q: Did your husband have any 'Christian' influence in your marriage?

A: *He continued to go to church but would never pray or read the Bible with me. I led family worship, but mostly when he was not there, as he would not listen, and therefore I felt it was not encouraging the children to listen. He would often tell me off for teaching the children catechism, or encouraging them to learn scripture. I sometimes accused him of being jealous of God, as he did not like me praying for he said I should be talking with him, not God.*

Q: Did your husband go to church with you?

A: *He only went to church on Sunday mornings, and was very critical of all the Christians in church. He still attends church, and says he is a Christian, but I think it is more about him feeling he is 'doing the right thing' and he would say this. He has never renounced his faith. What I found upsetting, however, was the way he used the Bible against me, telling me that he could tell me what to do because he was the head of the family, or tell me what to wear as he wanted me to be modest.*

Q: If there was no violence, what kind of abuse did you suffer?

A: *It was mostly subtle and continuous psychological abuse that was very controlling. For example, in terms of how he spoke to me, it would* *make me feel like I was a child. I explained this to him once, that he made me feel small and insignificant. He did not seem to care. He would not let me speak until he had finished saying his piece, and would then 'allow' me to. At this point I would seldom feel I had anything I wanted to say. I had to filter what I said, as he would be so critical of my opinions. I remember the day I decided not to tell him anything important to me anymore. We were in the kitchen, and he told me not to speak until he had finished speaking, He then raised his hand indicating that I could now speak. I felt really upset, and just like a small child to him. I said I no longer had anything to say. I felt as if he just trampled on my dreams and thoughts, and I decided that he no longer had the privilege of hearing them.*

My life consisted of trying not to upset him. If I upset him he would not speak to me, sometimes for weeks at a time. I became better at not upsetting him but felt as if I lost myself in the process. I felt plastic, not real. I would cook his favourite foods, kiss him when he got in from work, make sure that the house was tidy, the chairs tucked in under the kitchen table as he liked them to be. The car would pull in each evening and I would be frightened, hoping that there was nothing for him to be upset about. I didn't ever feel the situation would improve.

Q: Were you beginning to think it was not a normal marriage?

A: *I felt that I had 'normal' marriage difficulties, therefore nothing to complain to others about. I had decided when I first married that I would not complain about my husband, so I did not.*

Q: You mention being 'frightened'. Was fear a major factor in your relationship?

A: *Yes, I was afraid, but it's hard to know what I was afraid of. I was afraid of him going into a mood as then I had to work hard to get him out of it. I was afraid of his behaviour in front of other people, that he would be rude and I would feel embarrassed. A couple of times his* anger exploded, and I did think he was going to hurt me. It was more a mind game thing though. My fear was really relating to the mind games. He would use things that were important to me against me. He knew my faith was important so he would say that as a Christian I should behave in certain ways. It's the feeling that you could get into trouble at any time that makes you fearful. The fear felt quite abstract. I felt like he could kill me at the end, but in honesty don't think he would have.

Q: Can you elaborate on the psychological abuse you suffered?

A: *Yes, but so much of his behaviour was subtle. He would listen in on my phone conversations, following me round the house. He put a tracker on my phone, so he would 'know I was safe'. If we argued, he would follow me round the house not letting the argument end until I was in tears. Once he became very angry after I had answered the phone to someone from church that he didn't want to speak to. He called me names and I barricaded myself in the spare room. But he apologised the next day and I forgave him. He once forced me to have sex with him, but again was upset following my expression of unease, saying he didn't mean it to happen. Again, I forgave him, although weeks later when I told him I felt the way we had sex made me feel like I was being raped, he got angry and stopped speaking. It made me wonder how sorry he had really been. I think the abuse was mostly psychological but it was distressing, controlling and abusive.*

Q: How long did this abuse go on for?

A: *This went on for 15 years. I thought it was normal married life, not happy, but not unusual. He could be really kind, funny, buy me lovely things, take me away for weekends. But underneath it all I feared him, feared his moods, what he thought of me. Lots of this behaviour felt quite normal to me, as I never spoke of it to anyone. To speak about it would have felt as if I was betraying my husband. It* *was only when I spoke to others (and listened to the storyline of The Archers in the BBC Radio 4 Programme!), that I began to see that my marriage was dysfunctional. I didn't ever feel the situation would improve. But I felt that I had 'normal' marriage difficulties, therefore nothing to complain to others about.*

Q: Did your ex-husband succeed in isolating you?

A: *I was actually not that isolated. It was one of the things that I saw in my relationship as being wrong and I did fight against it. He tried to isolate me in quite subtle ways, telling me he only needed me, and could not understand why I needed other people. But I knew I needed them. Admittedly, I did not see as much of my family as I wanted but did see my friends in the day when my husband was at work. He wanted us to move to a rural location away from my friends, but I did say no, as this really concerned me. Having young children, running a toddler group at church and having evangelistic Bible studies with some of the mums meant I made lots of really good friends. As this was in the daytime, it was outside his control. I also worked two days a week and had good friends at work. Much of my emotional support has come from my kind work colleagues. I am wary of Christians who discourage women from working outside the home.*

Q: Am I right in thinking you tried hard to keep your marriage going?

A: *That's right. I tried hard to keep going in my marriage, to keep my husband happy, to be in many ways the 'perfect' wife. I did not believe divorce was permissible, so I had to keep going. But looking back I should have raised the fact that his behaviour was unacceptable. I should have stood up to him more. However, I don't think this would have made much difference. But I did feel when I finally left that he had had no warning. It was this that made me feel I had not tried hard enough. But once I 'saw' his patterns of behaviour to me* and his daughter, I could not 'un-see' them. By then it was too late. When I told people about it, and it was out in the open, I realised how dysfunctional my marriage was and how I was so scared of my husband.

Q: Did your ex-husband recognise that his behaviour was wrong?

A: *I don't think I could have ever made the marriage work as to this day he does not see that his behaviour was wrong. He sees the marriage breakdown being due to poor communication. But in the early days of our break up, my head felt as if I continually had a loop of thoughts that would move from 'I can't leave him, it's wrong, I can't break up my family' to 'I can't stay, I'm so unhappy'. When I was saying I would leave he was still being manipulative, threatening suicide, saying it would destroy the children. He would say I wasn't trying hard enough, and I would believe this. I found it hard to think straight.*

Q: The final 'push' for you in leaving the marriage then was the desperate need to protect your children. Am I right?

A: *You are right in that the final push was my children, especially my eldest daughter. I felt I was justified in leaving as I could see what it was doing to her. I really didn't want her to end up marrying someone like her dad. She's glad we're divorced. I felt I couldn't leave for me but could leave for my children. We're happy in my single parent family. I am happy being a single mother. I feel very protective over my daughter. His treatment of her makes me angry, whereas I have seldom felt angry about his treatment of me. The day I decided it was over was when he lost his temper with our daughter. I did tell him he had been out of order, but he said it was worth it as it 'shut her up'. Something clicked in my head that day.*

Q: Did you experience financial abuse?

A: *I knew very little about the finances but am not convinced this was abusive. I think it was something he used to make me feel I couldn't manage without him as I had never been involved with the money. I was anxious about spending too much money, but think that was part of the other behaviours, not something separate.*

Q: Why did you not tell close friends or relatives earlier about the abuse?

A: *I recently spoke with a friend who said that over ten years in a large church no-one had ever spoken to him or the congregation about domestic abuse. Yet from statistics alone there must have been many women and men in that church over the years for which this was a reality. This made me ask myself why I had never spoken to anyone in my church about it. The first time I spoke with any Christian about the abuse was when I had already decided to leave. At the point of leaving, I also left church, as I felt so hypocritical claiming to be a Christian and leaving my husband. I can think of several reasons why I did not speak to Christians about my marriage situation.* One reason *is that I believed divorce was only permissible in relationships where there was adultery. If I am honest, this made me wonder whether adultery would be a good way out of my marriage. I often wished my husband would leave me for someone else. I thought there was no way out of my marriage apart from this, so there was no point in my talking about my marriage difficulties, as it would not change anything.* A second reason *is that I believed wives should always submit to their husbands. I felt very guilty if I didn't want to do something my husband asked of me.* Thirdly, *I believed I should forgive all sins, and remain reconciled and thus remain in my marriage whatever happened to me.* A fourth reason *was that I felt inferior to my husband, due partly to the way I was treated.*

Q: Were there other reasons for not telling people about this abuse?

A: *To be honest, this feeling of inferiority I think was reflected in many of the blogs I read on biblical womanhood. I also think that churches give the impression of women being somehow inferior, even if this is not intended. I think I held these beliefs due to things taught in blogs and Christian books, and due to church teaching. It is not that what was taught in church was wrong. However sometimes the teaching is not balanced.*

Q: Do you still think that the teaching in your church was unbalanced?

A: *I still believe God designed marriage to be a lifelong commitment between a man and a woman. But if only this is taught, with no clear teaching on divorce, or acknowledgement that sometimes in our broken world divorce is better than staying in a damaging, threatening/ dangerous marriage, then it leaves people like myself trapped in situations that feel unsafe and even dangerous. The issue of women submitting to their husbands is another example. In the church I am now a member of, and love, men are often called to be leaders in their homes. However, I have never heard them called to love, cherish and honour their wives, and I have listened hard to hear this.*

Q: Tell us more about this, please?

A: *The subject of divorce does not seem to be preached in our churches, apart from in a condemning way. The church I go to does not appear to have a clear view on when divorce is valid. I had already begun divorce proceedings by the time I started going there but was told that if I had been attending when still married, I would have been encouraged to reconcile with my husband. I think looking back, that this encouragement would have led to me leaving church. I have forgiven my husband but feel very damaged emotionally by what happened in* *my marriage. To return to the marriage feels impossible for me. When I am told that this would have been the advice I would have been given, it feels as if my pastor does not understand how much I have been hurt. And I ask, what does the Bible really teach on the subject?*

I recently watched a video in which John Piper [2] says that a woman should endure 'verbal abuse', and 'endure a smack' from her husband. To me such teaching puts women at risk of staying in dangerous and harmful situations. If I had a friend who was in an abusive marriage I would tell her to leave, and not go back. For church leaders to encourage otherwise, to me, appears to neglect the women in their care and their safety.

Q: What pushed you in the end to leave your husband?

A: *I think I may have continued putting up with my abusive marriage partner beyond the fifteen years. I believed I was married until one of us died. I looked forward to being unmarried in heaven. The situation changed however when I started noticing his behaviour to my oldest daughter. He would continually criticise her, tell her she smelt, shout at her. One day he lost it, yelling at her. She was only twelve. My son closed his bedroom door and said 'Daddy loves us not her.' I then noticed that when her father was not being cruel, she would hug him, tell him she loved him. She was behaving like me. I hated it. I didn't want her to think that is what men are like. So, I told him I was unhappy, and that I wanted us to divorce. Initially he was repentant, said he would change, join a Bible study group, read the Bible (he never had, and discouraged me from doing so). But this did not last.*

Q: What happened then?

A: *After six months of counselling and talking, I moved out. Prior to this I felt very frightened of him. Moving to my own house and being*

---

2   *http://arewomenhuman.me/2010/08/08/john-piper-wives-should-endure-abuse-for-a-season/*. Although part of his advice here is questionable, Piper qualifies the statement by saying that if it was regular or severe then the church should be informed.

able to lock my door each night gave me such joy. I left church at this point as well. I felt so hypocritical, and that I was disobeying God. I read books on marriage and attended seminars in which I heard that 'marriage is difficult, it's a gym for our sanctification'. So, I thought that my marriage was no different. I think sometimes I did wonder whether things for me were worse than for others but knew that once I brought it into the open it would feel 'real', there would be no going back, I would have to deal with it one way or another. There were people inside and outside the church who I could have spoken to, but I didn't particularly feel I had anything to say.

Q: In which ways has domestic abuse 'damaged' you?

A: *The 'damage' keeps showing up in my life but it is gradually improving. When I first left I felt constantly frightened and paranoid. It was a constant feeling of panic. I became depressed within a year of leaving the family home, and felt suicidal, I felt I had no future at all, and was overwhelmed by guilt. I thought maybe I should return to my husband but felt I could never get back into bed with him. I find it hard to make decisions, to trust my instinct or opinion. I find it difficult to know what is 'true' in a situation. I find it hard to 'read' situations as I feel I 'read' my marriage wrong. My husband could be kind and cruel. I find that hard to make sense of. In general, my mood is now better, and anxiety is not always there, but I still have days when I can't shift the feeling of panic inside me, and battle with feelings of guilt and depression.*

Q: Are you positive about the future?

A: *The damage is improving. I feel optimistic about my future. My church is made up of several 'gospel communities'. These are small groups which meet each week, and we are encouraged to support the people within them. I feel very supported in this group, and feel also able to support others, which helps me. I am much less emotionally* *unstable than I was. Others can help me by being my friend, praying for me, loving me. I have had counselling, which was helpful when I was particularly depressed. But now I think I have to keep at the things we should all be keeping at. Reading the Bible, praying, meeting with Christians, meeting with friends, looking after my body – I run and find that it helps.*

Q: Can you say more about your feelings of 'guilt'?

A: *I feel guilty most days. I feel guilty for upsetting my husband, not keeping my promises, that he doesn't know what to do on Christmas day, that his life has not turned out how he wanted it to. I don't think these thoughts are things I should feel guilty about, but I do anyway. The guilt is false, but it is there anyway. I don't feel guilty about breaking up my family, in terms of the children living mostly with me. Our home is happier than it was when we were all together. God has been good to us. Some days I feel like the guilt is crushing me. Those days I preach hymns and Scripture to myself, and pray, which helps. The panic feelings can come from memories, and I have to remind myself that that is the past not now. I wonder whether the guilt is partly my personality. I really hate to think of anyone being sad.*

If a friend was sad then I would want to make it better. It feels odd when my ex-husband texts me to tell me something sad, and I feel responsible, and want to make it better, or help, but can't. I feel really sad when I think that he is sad, even though I know that he was unkind to me. My feelings do not really make logical sense and feel connected to my abusive relationship. It would be helpful if I could completely cut contact with my ex-husband, but we have children, so I can't.

Q: Do you regard divorce as a stigma?

A: *I don't feel that divorce is a stigma, and don't think I feel a failure now, although I did initially. When I felt I could not stay married in* *such an abusive relationship, I did feel I had failed God. I have moved on in my thinking from this now.*

Q: Is there anything else you'd like to add?

A: *I am not angry with God. I can see His hand in my life and in my marriage. I am thankful to Him for His faithfulness to me and know that my sadness makes me lean on Him.*

Louise is helping women in church and in society who are suffering domestic abuse. Like Rita, her experience of abuse enables her to empathise with others in need.

Key words used by Louise include:

'fear', 'frightened', 'damaged', 'guilt', 'panic feelings', 'unhappy', 'controlling', 'critical', 'angry', 'subtle', 'mind-game', 'distressing', 'manipulative', 'threatening', 'inferiority', 'panic' and *'crushing'*.

POSTSCRIPT

Before closing this chapter, I want to refer briefly to three other examples of domestic abuse. I could tell you, for example, of **Henrietta** whose marriage turned into a nightmare of domestic abuse. I remembered her becoming a Christian. She married a young man who appeared to be a keen Christian. The abuse inflicted on her by the husband was unimaginable. Towards the end of her marriage relationship, my wife and I pleaded with her to leave her violent husband because her life was in imminent danger. Eventually she did.

Mary, too, suffered abuse from the early days of her marriage and it eventually ended in unusual drama: 'the abuse doesn't have to win', she says, 'God was always there with me... he saved me from being killed many times.'

Lynn met her husband Ryan in church where he was a popular member so when Lynn and Ryan announced their engagement, the church people were delighted. Lynn also thought she had met the man of her dreams. Early in the relationship he slapped her in an argument which shocked Lynn but Ryan cried, offering an excuse. A few months later he slapped her again but this time Lynn asked for a divorce. His response was to threaten to kill her if she pursued a divorce. Things got worse and she was forced often to have sex. Finally, Lynn decided to seek the pastor's help so Ryan was called in too for counselling. Ryan denied everything and the pastor concluded that the devil was attacking the marriage so Lynn should stay in the marriage and Ryan was left unchallenged! Here is the familiar story of the abuser's image in public and church being so different from that at home. The abuse worsened and Lynn had thoughts of shooting or stabbing Ryan but decided against it. To make matters worse, everyone in the church imagined she was the problem in the marriage. There was no one she could turn to in church for help. In desperation, she contacted her brother who rescued her from immediate danger and harm.[3]

In the next chapter one woman who was trapped in an abusive marriage relationship with her pastor-husband tells her story, providing further evidence that an abuser can be a regular church adherent or even a church pastor yet abuse his wife and children. Such abusers are living a lie.

ACTION POINTS

1. Compare and contrast the domestic abuse suffered by Rita and Louise. Are there lessons to learn from their experience?

2. In what ways can domestic abuse 'damage' the victim? Illustrate your answer from Louise's story.

---

3   See 'It's Not Your Fault': True Stories of Abused Women, William H. Joiner Jr. (2015).

7. Victim: Charlotte
– A Pastor's Wife

Here is a detailed account of domestic abuse experienced by a pastor's wife. She wanted to honour the Lord in her life, marriage and family. Instead, she suffered years of cruel abuse.

OUTLINE

- Charlotte married a pastor when she was nearly twenty years old.
- Her husband-pastor exercised an influential biblical ministry and was held in high esteem.
- For twenty years of marriage she was 'controlled' by her husband.
- The abuse was almost entirely emotional, humiliating, threatening, financial and coercive involving isolation from friends and family.
- The children suffered and witnessed some of the abuse.
- The last five years of marriage involved relentless abuse alongside extensive physical violence at a time when he was having an extra-marital affair.
- The church knew nothing of their pastor's abusive behaviour. Charlotte was too afraid to report it.
- There was little choice for her in the end but to separate and divorce.

- The lies her husband told church members and eventually others outside the church isolated and disappointed her further.

Charlotte now tells her story for the first time.

EARLY DAYS

I married before my twentieth birthday while a student. The man I was marrying was unwilling to wait until I'd graduated and wanted me to give up my university course as he felt I had no need of qualifications to be a mother. My place was in the home; he didn't then believe that wives should work. He would be the main provider and that was how we were to live. My family were unhappy about this so there was much stress over the decision. Despite opposition, however, I completed my University course after marrying but I was now in a relationship where there was no scope to make decisions myself. I easily accepted that I was fortunate to have met him, someone who was happy to take responsibility for me and who would care for me - this is what I was being told. His authority over me was for my own good. He told me daily that I could never cope on my own, and he eventually made me very nervous around people as he always criticized everything I said or even how I laughed. This he usually conveyed after people had gone or by the angry way he'd look at me when they were still there. Sometimes he'd call me out of the room to tell me off, or in some cases tell anyone who was with me to go away as he wanted to speak to me alone. Being young and newly converted I easily became submissive.

CONTROL

He circumscribed my life in a way that was stifling and I became unable to make any decisions spontaneously. If a neighbour asked me and the children, to accompany her to a local park,

I couldn't. There were no escape routes as he was working at home. It was very demeaning to make an excuse or say that I'd have to ask. If I did something without asking, saying I thought it was better/useful/appropriate ... he'd say, 'it's not for you to think, it's for you to do – women can't think!' The control grew incrementally and looking back I diminished as a person. Gradually I was almost confined to the kitchen, especially if someone came to see him. I was expected to bring refreshments and leave the room, unless he needed to make an escape when people were staying too long! This I accepted as it became a happy solution not to have him watch over me. But after the break-up of the marriage, church members said they had never had the opportunity of getting to know me and concluded that I was very reserved. They knew me only through what he said about me.

OTHER PROBLEMS

There were other problems in the early years. My husband accepted a pastorate for some weeks overseas. I joined him later, having travelled from Britain with a toddler and a thirteen-day old baby. When I arrived, I realised that something was wrong as he wasn't interested in the children and had no time for us. The evening of my arrival, I asked him why he seemed so distant and cold. His response was that he had enjoyed freedom for the previous weeks and did not want the anchor of the children and myself anymore. I was devastated. I soon realised he was having an affair with the wife of an office bearer whilst her husband was away. He often telephoned and whispered on the phone when I was in another room. The stay there was traumatic. He went very often to visit a terminally ill lady who was supposedly staying in this woman's house. I was told years later that the woman wasn't staying there at all and certainly wasn't sick! When I had proof of the affair he threatened that should I tell anyone he would disappear, taking the children with him. This threat I believed, as a relative of his had done exactly that, when his wife was in hospital having their third child. I didn't tell anyone, although some friends there insinuated things about his behaviour; I didn't want to know anything, which would confirm or add to what I already knew. When I visited friends there, some years after our divorce, I was told that he had promised this woman he would return to her, even if it took him 'til he was ninety! During that temporary pastorate, he belittled me in front of her. I tried to be gracious to her but also tried keeping away from her. This remained a secret until another affair eighteen years later destroyed our marriage. Recovering from this episode was slow and I was depressed although no one noticed outside the home. I wanted him to apologise so we could make a new start. He refused, saying that David's response had been, 'against Thee, Thee only have I sinned'- it was nothing to do with me, though I was his wife.

FINANCE

He controlled the money completely and gave me a monthly allowance to buy food. This I accepted as he was earning a very small salary and initially I wasn't allowed to work. When we had more money and I was earning more than him, his absolute control over money didn't change. The school near our home was short-staffed and the headmaster begged me to help out. Once my husband saw how easily he could change his car with my salary, he changed his mind about my working! However, it always unsettled him. If I was employed for any length of time he would become really cross as I left in the morning and make it difficult for me, so that I would often be in tears going to work. He would insinuate there was someone on the staff I liked and would say things to destroy my confidence. He sometimes telephoned me in school and further upset me. There was no area of my life over which he didn't dominate. I would be taken to school and picked up even when I had my own car. In later years when required to stay late in school, he would check who else was there and sometimes question other members of staff.

After we'd been married two or three years my mother started giving me money regularly saying that it was important for me to have a little money of my own. She probably sensed the situation although nothing had been said. There was huge stress over this money as he wanted me to put it in the joint account saying we should have all things in common. As the money grew, I didn't want to keep it in my purse or tucked in a cupboard, I asked if I could put it in the post office for safe-keeping. This he couldn't cope with. I always had to ask permission to spend it even though he knew the money was given by my parents. Permission was not easily given.

CLOTHES

There was the same control if I asked for an item of clothing, he'd question whether I needed it, even if I used my parents' allowance. I had to ensure I sought permission when he was in a good mood; even then he would need time to think about it. Many of my clothes therefore were cast offs. The same was true of clothes for the children although it was easier to plead their cause. However, the obstacles before buying were just as trying and the clothes scrutinized when I brought them home. He often disapproved and I would have to return them to the shop because I was teaching them to be vain or some such complaint. He would give me a huge row in front of the children making them feel that they were also to blame. Looking back, I can see that I lived in bondage but I learnt to live in contentment, believing the Lord had chosen my lot in life and that no one else could have lived with him. I derived a lot of pleasure from being a mum and made a career of it, cooking the best food, reading to the children, helping them with homework, piano practice and many other things.

LIES

In addition to lying where he was going when he had an 'affair', he also made claims about my ill health and someone attending an evangelical church near my parents' home told my mother that she was so sorry for him as he had a wife who was crippled! The elders, when dealing with the break-up of our marriage, told me that he often said he had to help me out of bed and help me to dress. I only had sciatica and violent migraines occasionally but no major health problems – the migraines stopped immediately I moved from the marital home!

UNKIND

He couldn't cope with my being ill. When I had a migraine, and had to lie down for a few hours, he would show displeasure and leave the house to go visiting, even in the morning, which was not his usual habit. I fainted one Sunday morning and the last words I remember hearing as I faded into darkness was 'you can't faint now as we've got to get to church.'

I had to have cortisone injections on one occasion, but he was furious when I returned from hospital as he had told me not to have them. He didn't speak to me for days as I had disobeyed. I'd had to wait at the hospital having had local anaesthetic to my hands and would have had difficulty driving home immediately, but his work was too important for him to accompany me. He displayed the same attitude when the youngest child had eaten something in the garden, which could be regarded as a poison. He was angry because he had to leave his study to take us to hospital. He left us there; she was rushed by ambulance to another hospital and the next time I saw him was when he arrived home from prayer meeting that evening. After spending a day at the hospital, without food or drink and with a migraine, I had to take two different buses home, after first getting my daughter off to sleep and leaving her there. A young girl, living on a rough council estate nearby, seeing how ill I was, helped me on the bus. Her kindness was so amazing and unexpected.

INTRUSION

The intrusion into every part of my life was very difficult. I couldn't have the radio on as it would disturb him in the study; he'd hear me switch the kettle on and shout 'you're at that coffee again!' Gradually but firmly my personality changed and I became a 'doormat', only doing things at his behest. It was very difficult to arrange to have my hair cut at a time which wouldn't impinge on his day's programme; there was interrogation of why I needed it. Who was paying for it? Didn't I know he liked long hair and that long hair was biblical? Even when I'd negotiate time, he would usually plan to see someone or for someone to come for lunch and I would have to cancel my appointment. This pattern was constant.

Reading was frowned on in actuality, although ideologically commended. When I read a secular book, usually a biography of historical importance, he would say at length he had a study full of books I should read, but when I borrowed one he watched carefully how I handled it, or where I put it down – the criticism and stress were too much. I would hide a book on the far side of the bed and when he was out lie on the floor to read, then hide it again when I heard him coming in.

PHYSICAL VIOLENCE

The domestic abuse I experienced can be divided into two sections.

The first was emotional, psychological and spiritual abuse covering approximately the first twenty years of marriage; a lonely time of adjusting to living with someone who dominated my life completely. The second, during which time my husband was having an affair with a member in the church he pastored, covered about five years and the abuse was relentlessly physical. The transition from one to the other was very difficult as he had rendered me almost too lacking in confidence to do something as simple as answering the telephone. For years, I was expected to account for every minute of my day, then suddenly, I wasn't needed. He wanted the children and me out of the way. I was no longer on a leash and the 'freedom' was agoraphobic.

When our eldest child was in the last year of school and preparing for A level exams my husband began an affair with a church member and it was at this time that physical abuse began. These were very difficult and lonely years because I felt that no one should know as he was still preaching and I was hoping it was something he would work through as he had done earlier in our marriage. It soon became obvious that he would not give up the affair. He would eventually talk about our future apart and later in terms of one of us dying, saying things like, the only way out was for one of us to die, as being Christians, we couldn't divorce and that he certainly wasn't going to die as he had too much to live for.

There were daily problems and deceit, but it became obvious that his female friend was coming to the house regularly while I was at work. It was increasingly difficult to cope emotionally and I dreaded going to church as they would be watching each other all the time and finding time to be together or passing notes to each other. Another difficult feature of the relationship was her continuously telephoning the house. When much of the physical abuse was occurring no one knew, but bruises on my face and arms drew attention and I eventually had a broken nose, which required surgery and people found out. When the solicitor saw my bruised face, he said I needed a court injunction as most murders happened within a domestic environment; this gave me protection for a number of months. I was knocked unconscious at least twice and had a broken collar-bone as he used to pick me up and throw me. Frequently he would kick me when I was taking books to the car in the morning ready for school. My legs were permanently bruised.

On one occasion when I'd returned from meeting the church elders, my husband asked where I'd been and when I told him, he started pushing me around the kitchen whilst holding me by the throat. He was whispering to me that I was of the devil and that he could do anything he liked with me. I tried calling calmly to my children who were upstairs, along with my daughter's boyfriend. Initially they didn't respond because they were ashamed for the boyfriend to see. When I shouted more urgently for help again they all ran downstairs and while the boyfriend was trying to calm my husband down and telling him to take his hands off me, my youngest daughter was fainting. I had to call on one of them to see to her as I was still in his grip. When I was first knocked unconscious he seemed very nervous and had me to sit by him. He said a few times, 'Don't you ever make me do that to you again', implying it was my fault and this is what being constantly abused makes you feel. You feel like a child who deserves to be punished. You also feel too ashamed to tell anyone. It's the reverse of the buzz one has from feeling loved.

Another time, seeing me on a chair in order to reach something from the back of a cupboard he caught hold of my sweater and just threw me to the floor saying I shouldn't be standing on chairs. When I was playing a piano duet with my daughter he 'accidentally' knocked me off the chair and kicked me out of his way when I was on the floor. He sometimes manoeuvred me out of the house and locked me out for some hours – in winter, in slippers and light clothes. When my youngest daughter tried to pass me a scarf through the window he sent her to bed. One evening I walked a few miles in the locality as I didn't want to be seen by neighbours. I returned to the house and my daughter when I knew he'd gone to the prayer meeting. This was one of many such occasions. There were major things happening daily, both physical and emotional. I learnt to leave some money and phone numbers buried in a hole in the garden, because once, when we were in the house on our own, he hit me so badly that I had to leave in a hurry. It was in the middle of the night; I was so stressed I couldn't remember any phone numbers. Another time I had to run from the house in bare feet and walked about two miles to a friend's home. My husband would sometimes stand in the door of a room he'd manoeuvred me into and threaten me at length or just pick me up and throw me.

OVERDOSE

I was eventually driven to take an overdose as I was finding life so difficult and didn't know of a way out. I didn't want our doctor to know my husband was having an affair because he had shown much interest in the church. When I asked him for tranquilisers he refused saying I needed to talk to someone if I had problems. Over a period of time I acquired tablets. My husband stood over me as I took them, taunting me that I was too much of a coward to take them. It was a Sunday morning and I always found going to chapel difficult, as his woman friend would be there. He was also happy on a Sunday as he was seeing her for much of the day. I was at the edge of despair, knowing he wanted me out of the way. He insisted that I drive myself in my old car to church as, in his words, I looked fine. In the providence of God, I arrived safely but collapsed as I was making my way to my seat. That evening when I recovered consciousness he was very angry and said he was ashamed to be living with a murderer.

SPIRITUAL ABUSE

He often tried to convince me I was an unbeliever and that by him driving me out of the house it would be, for him, a biblical situation of the unbelieving partner leaving. He told me that once I left he would open all the windows and let the devil out. According to him there was a smell of evil in the house, which he wanted to be rid of.

EVENTUAL HELP

The help I eventually had, was of great value; without it I would not have survived. I told a deacon who, along with his wife, was a close family friend. He was the first person I confided in and was of immense help to me, as the situation was getting out of hand. Months later he and his wife joined us on holiday and I realised he hadn't even told her, proving to me he was the correct choice. Eventually, my husband became suspicious that I was confiding in him and by then his wife too and would confront him about what I'd told him. As he was such a careful person he decided it was best I didn't confide in him anymore. Some months before I was aware of the affair, my husband had told his friend's wife that he had fallen for someone else. She eventually told her husband who could see I was losing weight so he asked a church member, a professional lady and family friend, to keep an eye on me. She was a great help both emotionally and practically. A very discreet and unemotional person who knew what questions to ask. She would bring me home from church on a Sunday evening as I needed to avoid the coffee time when my husband and his female friend would be finding opportunities to be together. This friend took me to the hospital when my nose was broken and once or twice, when I had been badly beaten she 'happened' to call at the house, apparently noticing that my husband's car was in her street as he would call with close friends living there. One of these occasions was after he had knocked me unconscious and his story to them, apparently was that he, poor thing, was so upset because he'd shouted at me and that as a result I'd fainted.

One thing I found important was to have someone believe my story; 'to trust yourself when all men doubt you' is difficult. I took her provision to be providential, even in her no-messing, non-emotional temperament. She also very kindly gave me a key to her home as a refuge to which I fled many times. For her immense generosity of heart, a private, independent person, I am grateful and thank God for providing her; she would not utter a word to anyone and now when I meet her she never refers to that time.

SELF-APPOINTED EXPERTS

When the church elders knew about the situation and dealt with the breakdown of the marriage they apparently questioned my husband and later asked him if they could speak to me. He declined, saying he wanted to protect me. I disagreed, as I felt they had a right to know. My husband believed I wouldn't be willing to see them, as I was timid and he had always told me, 'no one will listen to you, they know that you're mentally deranged'. He was able to humiliate me, taking advantage of my reluctance to expose him. I believe now, in retrospect, that the Lord gave me much courage and resolve. A meeting with the elders was arranged.

I had struggled to cope with my husband's extra-marital relationship secretly for three years and had concluded there was no turning back. Once the church members knew, some individuals set themselves up as 'experts' and felt they could change the situation. Some called at the house to speak to us; one insisted that, in front of him, I should kiss my husband which was the very last thing I wanted to do. Another evening I was called out of bed to see a member of the congregation who fell on his knees before me and kissed my hand saying 'please, please don't do this to your lovely children'. The irony was that he too was having an affair at the time and subsequently left his wife! One lady who attended the church telephoned and told me I needed psychiatric help. I had letters from many others. With all these I listened and did not tell them anything. My G.P. had suggested: 'keep your dignity, don't share your problems with people in the church' and in hind sight I'm glad I didn't. There were some members of the church, who believed my husband and they, when out shopping or in parent evenings at my child's school, ignored me. They eventually found out the truth about the situation but it took them three years; years which were very difficult for me and especially for the children. It was also a huge disillusionment for them as they had trusted him when others by now had turned against him.

EXTERNAL INTERVENTION

When I had both begun legal proceedings for divorce, another difficult situation arose with huge implications for my confidence and wellbeing. A local minister of the gospel wanted to interview us separately in order to make a statement to evangelical ministers concerning our marriage. On two occasions, I met with two ministers for several hours; they concluded I was lying about the affair, that I hadn't been an adequate help-meet for my husband and that, as a Christian, I shouldn't have a divorce but a judicial separation. I felt so humiliated. There were immediate repercussions to these sessions. Not only was I feeling wronged and abused by my husband and his friends but now there was an official line taken against me and an unjust verdict was being passed. I regretted not having taken someone with me. The meetings with the ministers had a deep, lasting effect on me as one of them had known the family for many years and had been to our home for meals. He appeared to be a caring man, but on this occasion, was very aggressive in his accusations, only confirming my feeling I was inadequate and that the abuse was in response to this inadequacy. The evangelical world had supported my husband wholeheartedly without knowing the facts. I was ostracised. Ministers who had visited our home and had hospitality ignored me. Many came to the house at my husband's invitation to hear his side of the story but they never asked to see me. My husband also asked two prominent preachers to write a letter to the church officers saying that I was mentally deranged. One of them hadn't seen me for years and another was almost part of the family and we all loved him dearly. Both apologised when my husband married the woman he'd been having an affair with and one said that it would be a regret he'd carry to his grave that he had believed my husband and his many lies. All this scarred me for years and I had difficulty respecting ministers.

LEGAL INTERVENTION

It was very difficult for a sheltered Christian to be thrown into the world of divorce with the associated legal wrangling. Also,

I was losing my husband to a person who was in the same church and I felt I was being thrown out on to the mercy of the world, which was very frightening.

The worst aspect of it all, however, was the betrayal and deceit by someone I had really thought would be my rock, against external agencies. This was also a stark reality for our children. They had been brought up strictly and were not allowed to participate in social events with their school friends. Yet their father did things their school friends were never exposed to. I certainly didn't want to involve the church now I was on a legal trajectory lest I tarnish it by association, yet the wife of an elder said, in response to my telling her that I was seeking legal advice, 'we wouldn't have come with you this far just to leave you now'. This was heart-warming and reassuring.

TRAUMATIC

Visiting the solicitor was traumatic. My husband told me that he had a solicitor and that I should seek one, so that he could go ahead with the divorce. This was a lie and when my solicitor's letter arrived he showed it to the children, blaming me for breaking up the marriage. This was one of many occasions when he tried to turn the children against me with lies and naturally for a few days they wouldn't speak to me. I couldn't tell anyone about this; it was a sensitive and volatile situation. My solicitor wanted me to have a court injunction when my husband broke my nose and it was a shock to have a Bible thrust in front of me and asked to swear on it. The shock of launching into this legal world was immense. *It would have been especially helpful to have had someone to talk me through it – a sounding board.* But in the situation, I was afraid to contaminate others with what was happening to me, and I lived in fear every day, just moving a step at a time. I had decided not to tell my family until the tale was out in the public arena as I didn't want pressure from any quarter. They would have immediately wanted me to leave, fearing for my safety. I didn't want to do things quickly as I had the children to consider and I wanted the situation to develop naturally.

Against this background life was lived fully; I didn't lose a day's work. I needed to be out of the house and with people who seemed to care. Both I and one of my daughters had surgery, the children had school and degree examinations while it was raging on. We all looked worse for wear, but with God's help we got through it. My husband turned everything around to blame others. There were countless episodes when the children saw things which upset them; he would turn it around and blame them. Likewise, we were getting a divorce because I had destroyed his love for me not because he was having an affair. The elders were being blamed for getting rid of him because of a power struggle and finally he made a speech announcing his resignation on account of church members gossiping, even though they had petitioned him to leave.

Providentially, people emerged to support me, and also the children, although I was actually daily facing the difficulty in the home on my own, and often felt completely isolated, unable to face the next few moments let alone the rest of my life. But this was unavoidable. *No pastor came anywhere near me and this I found difficult.*

KEY FACTORS

The key factors in helping me through the time of the affair was my choice of person to tell, one who, like me, was mindful of God's will and who would wait for matters to unfold naturally and for people not to find out by his mouth. I could call on him at any time. My dependence reached a point, when I looked for him in church in order to calm myself and he, realising this, would walk down the aisle a little, just so I could see that he and his wife were there. Also, the later emerging of my other friend who I knew had previously thought the world of my husband but believed he could be guilty. *There was someone else who wanted to be my confidante but who I couldn't have trusted. In her hands, I feel the outcome would have been quite different.*

Another thing which helped me and initially rose out of sheer desperation, was a notebook in which I copied hymns so that I could carry them with me and read or sing them to myself. I found it so helpful that it became a crutch and I took it with me everywhere. My husband destroyed it, and I believe it was his way of hiding evidence I was a Christian. When I sing those hymns now, they bring tears to my eyes and it's then I realise how far I've come and how much the Lord has really done for me, in keeping me and the children. I derived strength also from Spurgeon's Daily Readings but it came to remind me of this difficult time so I avoided it for years afterwards.

REFLECTIONS

This chapter seems preoccupied with myself but I am mindful that there was also a congregation of bewildered and confused people who were suffering spiritually if not emotionally, during part of this time. My experience is probably an extreme example and some victims may not be suffering in the same way. When I was a young Christian and newly married, I knew some couples whose marriages seemed similar to mine and whose husbands dominated their wives in a way I now feel to be excessive. At the time, they were our closest friends and I assumed it was the way Christian families functioned. As my circle of friends grew I saw that this wasn't true of all Christians. But my husband frowned on marriages where the wife's opinions and needs were respected and he maintained that they were the result of either a weak husband or a domineering wife.

Should I have told someone when the first affair occurred? Did my silence give him confidence that I wouldn't tell anyone subsequently, when he had another affair? Was I responsible for keeping an unworthy person in the pulpit, handling the most precious word of God? It's easy in hindsight to see that telling someone then could have been the correct action but I may also have been blamed for frustrating the Lord's purposes and seriously curtailing a man's preaching and pastoral ministry.

CONCLUSION

- The person I told was careful not to make the situation worse. I trusted him not to tell anyone. He also moved at my pace.
- Although he found the situation difficult to believe at first, he still trusted and respected me.
- Similarly, my lady friend had the same qualities of integrity and believed me, but she appeared eager to resolve the situation for my sake. The combination of both, in retrospect, was perfect.
- Both these people knew my husband well and were keen supporters of his ministry, yet recognised he could be guilty.
- They were capable of carrying a heavy burden without feeling the need to share. Many people share confidential details asking people to pray but it can be an excuse to gossip.
- There were elders who were equally competent, possibly more incisive and eager to resolve the situation who might not have moved at my pace.
- There are people to avoid speaking to.

- It would have helped me to know some of the decisions being made by the elders.
- I wonder at some point, whether it would be helpful to meet others in the same position. One's self esteem is so severely damaged it could be reassuring and healing to meet others. This would have been impossible during the abuse and would only have made the situation worse if he had found out.

POSTSCRIPT

These years were very lonely. However, support emerged from unexpected places. Months before the church were aware of our situation, I started working in a school which was new to me. The staff previously unknown to me were unusually lovely and supportive, without knowing my situation. Eventually I had to tell the headmaster and he was very understanding, though I sometimes arrived late at school because my husband stopped me using the car and I would have to cycle. He eventually advised me to tell the staff as I needed friends, and he was sure they would support me. One staff member was the wife of a minister in the area and she became a very close friend. Her husband and another minister, neither being of evangelical persuasion, often stood up for me when others said bad things about me and I had strength from their support and thank God for it.

This support was from outside the church. I didn't know what was being said within the church officers' meetings so I lived in a world of rumours and was often fed information by my husband, which was frightening. He gave me scare stories of what the office bearers thought and said about me, I had no one to share these fears with. There were times when I panicked because I felt I was being severely wronged and he was jingoistic in the support he was having. I felt that this support was a bad testimony to all around, to the head teacher who saw me bruised and emotionally broken, also for my wider family.

In fairness to the church members, I had amazing kindness from so many when I moved out of the marital home both practically in cleaning and painting and in gifts of furniture, duvets, plants etc. One deacon offered to come to the house to be a support on the day I moved. There have been other close friends who, in later years, have listened patiently when I've unburdened myself. They will never know how much this meant and how much I still treasure memories of such support.

THERE ARE ALSO WIDER IMPLICATIONS OF ABUSE.

Apart from the obvious effects, *there are implications for sin and forgiveness that are unresolved in my mind even today*. The question arises concerning its effects on one's spiritual life, long term, after it's all over and some of the scars have healed; essentially concerning one's relationship with God and ultimately one's effectiveness as a Christian. Does one forgive even though there has not been repentance and forgiveness is not sought? And if so, is that compromising justice? Forgiveness has to be felt from within and not merely rhetoric. What if, worse still, there's no inclination to forgive? In my life, I am where I am and am thankful for the amazing ministry, which in the providence of God I am now having.

A difficulty arose, in my mind, over taking communion. Initially I felt that the Lord would recover my husband and that he would repent. When I saw that he was determined to continue his relationship, my taking communion from him felt wrong as the woman with whom I had personal issues was also receiving communion. Refusing would make a statement about my life or our life as a couple and cause more inquiry from the church. When the deacons and elders knew about the problem I felt free to decline.

I have been in a spiritual desert for years, doubting God's love to me, but am now being restored. The desert years were not apparent as I maintained attendance at church, but it affected my relationship with God. In my heart, I was rebellious against the providences He was allowing in my life and I became very cynical. But I recognise and accept that it's from 'Heavenly Jerusalem's towers, the path through the desert' we trace and it is only then we will fully understand.

Key words used by Charlotte:

'control', 'bondage', 'intrusion', 'criticism', 'humiliated', 'lonely', 'lies', 'scared', 'betrayal', 'deceit', and 'isolated'.

The next chapter provides a striking contrast for it relates the experience of a pastor whose wife abused him for years.

ACTION POINTS

1. Write down any points in this story that disturb and challenge you.

2. How should the church leaders have responded in this situation? Give details for your answer.

8. Victim: Dan
– A Pastor

This chapter is necessary because no one should imagine that most pastors and church officers are guilty of domestic abuse. That is not true; the vast majority of them have happy marital relationships and are helpful models for their children and young couples in the church to follow. It is important therefore that we keep a balance and not assume that all or many men in church office are abusers.

This chapter is also necessary because it redresses the balance in reminding us that a pastor, elder, deacon or other male church worker may be a victim of domestic abuse rather than being an abuser. This may shock you. We need, however, to be open to the possibility. It is impossible to know how many church officers are victims of domestic abuse because they normally keep the abuse secret. The number may be small and personally I only know of a tiny number of pastors who are abused. It is difficult to grasp the stark reality that these men are abused– cruelly and psychologically – by their wives. The abuse is normally hidden from the church with the husband preferring to suffer and lovingly protect his wife while trusting God and praying for an improved marriage relationship. Sadly, the latter rarely occurs.

In this chapter, we read about a U.K. pastor of a large evangelical church who suffered domestic abuse for years yet continued to love his wife, longing for a closer relationship with her. There are several reasons why this pastor, referred to as Dan, is sharing his story here for the first time.

- A major reason is to help male victims; their voice is often ignored.
- He is also eager to alert church leaders to the fact that men in churches can suffer extensively at the hands of their wives, even though they may be church officers.
- Wives too can be devious and 'controlling' and in such a way that the public cannot see.
- Dan acknowledges that in evangelical churches more women are trapped by controlling men. But he adds that even in complementarian churches like the one he led, abusive behaviour can often be reinforced and tolerated by questionable views on subjects like divorce. He claims it is by no means a one-way street.
- Another reason for sharing his experience is his desire for churches to be wise, sensitive, fair and biblically pastoral in approaching such cases. Too often, the husband is not believed, even if he is a pastor who has served the church well. His claims to be the victim fell on deaf ears and the abuser remains a respected, popular member of the church!

His story is told in an interview format below; it is told, however, with considerable sadness, disappointment and honesty. He remains heart-broken over what has happened and needs prayer.

INTERVIEW[1]

Dan

Q: Tell us briefly, Dan about your family background.

A: *I'm from a non-Christian family. It was a very stable and happy home with a clear moral framework in which we could talk and share*

---

1   Email correspondence: November/December 2017 and January 2018.

openly about matters troubling us, including relationships ı
This ought to have stood me in good stead for my own relatioı

Q: *When did you become a Christian?*

A: *I became a Christian, like many others, while studying in University.*

Q: What did you do after leaving University?

A: *For a period of time I gained experience in business and then I worked for a parachurch ministry before becoming a church pastor.*

Q: Did you have a strong sense of call to the pastoral, preaching ministry?

A: *I was really persuaded that I wanted to be a pastor by the end of my studies in University. I thought, however, that it was important to have experience of secular work before entering the Christian ministry. I was then invited to be an elder in the church I attended. During this period, I had a continuing desire and clear conviction concerning ministry and this was endorsed by those in the church. The leaders and the congregation confirmed I was suitably gifted for the pastoral/ preaching ministry.*

Q: How well and for how long had you known your wife before marrying?

A: *We had known each other for four years before we married. I would have said that I knew her very well and thought I had a good understanding of her personality, character, struggles, hopes and dreams. Looking back now, I think that was very naïve and that, in reality, nobody is really allowed to know her at all. She has kept part of her life secret and locked for years with no one given access to it. Only later in the marriage did I discover this fact.*

Q: Tell us about your church ministry, without identifying its location.

A: *I pastored a large church in England for over ten years, a church which was always exciting to be at. We had a brilliant group of elders, young men and women training for ministry and Christian work, church plants happening almost each year, people being converted and baptised almost every month. There were lovely groups of Christian friends who I felt genuinely shared life's joys and sorrows together. I loved preaching and personal pastoral work and there was much of it to do. I believe I was genuinely appreciated and loved by the church family for my preaching ministry and pastoring work through the week.*

Q: During your ministry then, in which there was considerable encouragement and blessing, there was a marital problem that no one else knew about. Is that right?

A: *Yes, no one knew about it in the church. I did not tell anyone about it.*

Q: The marital problem was one of abuse on the part of your wife. Can you share a little about this please?

A: *Of course, though it is not easy. Essentially, the abusive element of the relationship was about the total refusal of intimacy and sex. That may sound silly in a marriage but it was a fact. And this fact led to 'control' in many other ways too. My wife controlled our relationship in so many different ways. For example, she insisted on us always holding hands in public in order to demonstrate what a perfect couple we were. That is only one example. But in private it was very different. Constantly she accused me of being obsessed with intimacy in marriage and that I should not expect 'any of that'. This message was particularly reinforced on occasions like anniversaries and birthdays or other special occasions.*

Q: Were you frightened of your wife?

A: *No, I wasn't ever frightened in my marriage. It was much more about being worn down. My wife exercised almost complete 'control'. One example is that I was expected to say exactly where I was going at all times and when I'd be back. Being even five minutes late may not lead to shouting but I would get told I was letting her down and that I was being inconsiderate and selfish. Money was another area where control was manifest. Although I did our family accounts, I would be in trouble if there was any evidence I'd bought things we did not need. One of my most vivid early marriage memories is being told how wasteful and selfish I was for buying a coffee from McDonalds when I was on my way home after working late. I was very tired and I needed a coffee to help me stay awake while driving home in the car!*

Q: Did anyone in the church or the wider family suspect something was wrong in the marriage?

A: *No. Anybody looking at our relationship from outside would have thought, because I'm physically bigger and much more extrovert, that, if anyone, I was the person in charge of our relationship. But at home it was not like that at all. I wasn't frightened. It was just a sense that life would be made unbearable through being ignored and an emotional withdrawal if I upset her at all, even in the most trivial way.*

Q: Your wife's public image in the church was one of respect and popularity. Was she involved in teaching individuals or groups in the church?

A: *Yes, she was respected and admired. By the time I was leading a large and growing church, I had to sit through marriage preparation classes where my wife would tell women how they needed to take notice of 1 Corinthians 7 and not deprive their husbands. Then I would go to bed knowing that even a touch would result in a rebuke.*

Q: Was your wife aware of what she was doing to you? Did she apologise?

A: *My wife never apologised! Perhaps the area that shows this most clearly is what happened after an argument or a disagreement. Whoever was at fault and whatever the fault was – and marital arguments are usually a bit on both sides! – I would be always ignored until I apologised, even though I may not have been at fault. I didn't realise it until after I had left the relationship but what this led to was my feeling continually anxious that I hadn't apologised enough for every little thing and feeling always on edge about it.*

Q: Did you consider leaving your wife early on?

A: *For the first few years, I really did not want to leave my wife because I loved her and cared for her. I also thought it would be morally wrong to leave her. I was also genuinely hopeful for change and prayed to this end. Then working for the church, I was busy and the emotional reward of the work helped to fill the vacuum which I felt at home.*

Q: Can I press you concerning the lack of intimacy in your marriage? This must have been a huge disappointment but my interest is in seeing the link with domestic abuse.

A: *I do not want to answer the question in great detail for obvious reasons. Needless to say, on our wedding day, I was in love and excited about being with my loved one until death parted us. I anticipated a close intimate relationship. After a couple of months, however, I was repeatedly told that I was ruining things and was obsessed by having a normal marital relationship. I was accused of being unreasonable. I was at fault, she kept telling me. If I say that the marriage was not consummated for nearly five years, you will understand how she controlled this aspect of our marital relationship but her control of our relationship extended to all other areas too. Feeling desperate at times, I had thoughts of annulling the marriage but I could not do it. And* *the reason was simply this: I really loved my wife. We had known fun times together but the relationship was becoming more difficult.*

Q: What steps did you take to improve the relationship?

A: *As the months went by, I stopped indicating that I'd like to kiss or cuddle her because I knew that she would say it was all my fault that she did not want to kiss me or be intimate with me. 'If you were nicer to me', 'if you bought me more flowers' or 'if you weren't...' The excuses were numerous and it was always my fault. Verbal abuse alongside constant accusations against me and rejection became regular features in the relationship. Eventually, during one argument, my wife disclosed the fact that she had been sexually abused as a child by a relative. I understood more then about her response to me and was sympathetic. When I suggested counselling or other help, she refused and claimed she did not have a problem with her past. The problem was with me!*

Q: Did your wife change her mind about seeing a counsellor?

A: *Yes, because there was another problem. My wife wanted us to have children. That is tricky especially if you are not in a real marital relationship and intercourse is prohibited. Eventually this provided some motivation for her to go to a qualified counsellor which later enabled us to conceive. I had hoped that this might be the beginning of a change, enabling her to think it may be desirable to have a normal relationship. That did not happen.*

Q: What did happen then?

A: *Once our first child was born it all got so much worse. I think husbands may sometimes feel ignored to some degree after the birth of a child as mothers, rightly and necessarily, give their time and energies to the baby. I understand that. But given how unloved, controlled and ignored I was already feeling, this only compounded it. There was also* *a strong sense on my part that all my wife had ever wanted was the image of a perfect Christian family and not really me at all. I felt she now had what she'd always wanted–and it was not me!*

Q: Can you give other examples of 'control' and abuse?

A: *For example, the control exercised by my wife meant that I even had to be watched washing my hands when I came in from outside. I was also told where to sit at meal time. These were just a few of the examples of the control she exercised. I would not even get a kiss on the lips unless I was physically leaving the house and therefore couldn't 'demand any of that.' I was always at fault. It was impossible to do or say anything right – at any time. I talked about telling someone how she talked to and about me and what was happening in our relationship. Her answer was calculating: 'No one would believe you'. Soon after the birth of our second child, I wanted to end the abusive relationship but I could not do it. Leaving a mother with a baby would have been cruel. Over the next seven years, however, I was gripped by fear, partly because of the things I was told by my wife that made me believe that no one would want me or believe my story.*

Q: Did you tell your wife you thought of leaving her?

A: *Yes, I did. After ten years, for the first time I talked to her about leaving. I explained that I was not happy and I knew she was not happy either. If we could not change things so that we actually had a marriage rather than a house-share with children we needed to stop this charade. Sometime later, I told my wife that unless she came to counselling and faced up to the issues involved that I would be leaving. Positively, she agreed to come to the counselling sessions. That was great, so I thought. Encouragingly, during many sessions she told the counsellor how sorry she was for all that had happened which had been her fault. She seemed genuinely repentant and I sensed there was hope for us. Sadly, however, there was no change at home. It was the* *same as ever with rejection, manipulation, control, verbal abuse and coldness.*

Q: Why did you not leave your wife earlier?

A: *As I look back, I do wonder a lot about this. Obviously, I really loved this woman who was my wife. Then once the children were born I had responsibilities and a love for them too. They were my children and important to us both. Another reason is because I just got used to this being my life, and I threw my energies into my church, my friends and my children. Nearer the end, it was mostly because I was afraid that if I left I would lose my family, my home, my job and my friends.*

Q: What pushed you in the end to leave your wife?

A: *As the pastor of a large church, I was in a controlling and abusive marriage for as long as 17 years. It was a long period and I struggled hard over these years to improve the marital relationship, seeking by God's grace to cope with the abuse. It was hard. After all the efforts, prayer, the many counselling sessions it was obvious that my wife refused to change and become less controlling. The decision was a painful one to make but I felt in the end there was no choice and I was being driven out.*

Q: Can you share some of the ways the Lord sustained and helped you during this long period of marriage and after leaving your wife?

A: *Sometimes I have felt that I could not go on physically and contemplated suicide. God in his grace stopped me acting on those thoughts. More often I have felt I can't continue spiritually and that there is… no hope. But somehow, I can't run away from the Lord, and the grace and kindness of Christ has always brought me back to a faith that often feels fragile but is, nevertheless, astonishingly comforting. When it all feels too much I just remind myself that I know Jesus loves* *me. The last sermons I preached at my church were on Job, and there was providence in spending time seeing how darkness doesn't preclude faith.*

Q: What happened when you left?

A: *When I left, all my fears came true. I lost my home and almost all my assets. I lost three quarters of my time with my children. My church fired me. All my sermons were erased from the internet. The church leaders wrote to me and told me I had behaved wickedly. My wife remains active in the same church. I am glad she is cared for by the church. I really am glad of that. However, this only compounds the sense of injustice I experience and it reinforces the impression to those who do not know the facts that it is all my fault.*

Q: Are you inferring that the church leaders did not listen to your story and check it out?

A: *I do understand that when a husband and pastor leaves the family home it is a fairly natural conclusion to draw that this is principally his responsibility. So I'm not too cross about the people who don't know the details assuming that, though I think a wider realisation that life is complex and things aren't always what they appear would be helpful. I don't think the church leaders were prejudiced as such, it was just easier for them to make it my fault as it avoided confrontation and meant they did not ever have to challenge my wife. And despite the fact that as a leader I had encouraged others on numerous occasions to think through the subject of divorce biblically and to study it in depth and had taught it in sermons, it seemed none of my fellow leaders had really grappled with it or, if they had, regarded it as just people trying to find excuses rather than serious attempts to grapple with the biblical text.*

Q: Are you able to share your disappointment in the way in which the church treated you and your claim regarding domestic abuse?

A: *One of the things I feel most sad about was the way Christians viewed me leaving the family. There was also quite a lot of spreading of 'news' (gossip) about me by leaders in the church to other people and to other church leaders. They were inclined to just believe and repeat things my ex-wife said without taking any trouble to question or check them with me. That was disappointing.*

When I sat with a church elder I'd worked with for 15 years and told him what happened, he told me that 'every marriage has its burdens'. Others said 'you know your children will be damaged…' and 'if you can't make your marriage work what chance is there for mine?' Despite the fact that the church leaders know the story, my ex-wife remains a church member and nobody has challenged her behaviour.

Q: Did you recognise during your marriage, that you were in an abusive relationship?

A: *Only one person, a very senior Christian leader, had the courage to tell me that my marriage had been abusive. To be honest, it has taken me two years since leaving my wife to be able to say that he was right. I now see that the woman who had been so awfully abused herself in childhood by a relative abused me in turn.*

Q: This may sound a silly question, but are you in a difficult position now?

A: Yes. I don't regret leaving my wife as such though that makes me sad. Some of the consequences of leaving especially around the children and friendships make me sad. I'm not good at being alone and feel very lonely quite often. I don't think I can ever be a pastor again, even though I'd love to but in the eyes of some I'd always lack the required character. But it was an impossible, controlling and abusive relationship for which I am being punished by Christians.

I've been following all the news over the past months about Harvey Weinstein and other well known men who abuse women. I realise that what I experienced in church was exactly what many of those women experienced; the fear that it would be me and not my abuser who would have to suffer loss of employment and being publicly shamed if I told the truth. Worst of all, the experience of just not being believed.

Q: Thank you Dan for sharing your sad experience. There is obviously a lot more you could share but would you like to add briefly some final words?

A: *Yes, I would. Please pray for me. I am only slowly recovering from an abusive marriage with all its consequences. It is not easy at all but my trust is in the Lord. If sharing my own experience here can help one or more persons avoid the situation I've been placed in then I will be encouraged.*

Key words used by Dan include:

'control', 'frightened', 'anxious', 'verbal abuse', 'rejection', 'ignored', 'manipulation', 'worn down', 'ignored', 'desperate', 'accusations', 'unloved', 'fear' and 'coldness'.

POSTSCRIPT: COMPLEXITY OF DOMESTIC ABUSE

Dan's story illustrates again that the subject of domestic abuse is complex as are the varying factors lying behind the abuse. One aspect which is not referred to often in Christian circles is the impact of childhood sexual abuse on a marital relationship. Childhood sexual abuse, often by a close relative or friend, can have a devastating effect on the male or female victim, although many do adjust to married life comfortably, with or without prior counselling.

What happens therefore when a young lady sexually abused in childhood by a relative over months or years is later bold enough to marry but without telling her prospective partner or seeking counselling and support regarding her painful past?

Sadly, the abuse suffered remains a hidden and closed part of the victim's life. For some, it is genuinely forgotten; for others it is kept hidden as a closely guarded secret yet the opportunity may arise for the person to confide in a friend or a counsellor. It is in this context you need to understand the preceding interview with Dan; his wife had suffered childhood sexual abuse then years later married but was unable to cope with the intimacy of marriage. Although loved by her Christian husband, she coped only by becoming an abuser herself and controlling her husband in all aspects of the relationship.

Having read Dan's story as the victim, it is appropriate for us to attempt to appreciate something of the trauma his wife suffered as a child and its effect upon her. We dare not minimise her pain and suffering over the years, although it may have been better if she had shared the secret with her fiancé before marriage. Did a sense of shame and the fear of losing her fiancé keep her from revealing that dark secret? Alternatively, a decision to receive professional counselling prior to considering marriage without telling her fiancé could also have been a positive step. In guarding her well-kept secret, she was being unfair to herself and to her marriage partner. The following pointers in understanding her abuse may be helpful and applicable to others in similar situations:

Casualty

Anyone, male or female, suffering sexual abuse in childhood is a **casualty**. The individual has suffered cruel and criminal behaviour, even if committed by a trusted relative. It is a crime which has a major impact on a person's life. Normally the major effect of the abuse is emotional/psychological and can sometimes be expressed behaviourally in distressing, often irrational, ways. Just as people with health problems need to consult a medical doctor urgently so those who have suffered sexual abuse need urgent and professional assistance in confronting their dark past. Expert help is available, though recovery may be slow. However, the fact is that any victim of abuse is a casualty suffering deep emotional pain and shame; help is needed.

Calamitous

Reinforcing the perspective of the victim as a casualty, the **calamitous** effects of abuse need to be recognised. Childhood sexual abuse is calamitous in many ways, involving deep, unimaginable distress for the victim; the abuse is like a black cloud overshadowing his/her entire life. They will feel confused, dirty, guilty and depressed amongst other things. Self-hatred in such circumstances is common while suicide may at times appear an attractive escape route. In pastoral work there needs to be a recognition of the calamitous effects of childhood sexual abuse on the individual.

Cocoon

In order to protect oneself and cope with life, a victim may become a **cocoon** in order to isolate and protect themselves from the memories and hurt involved in the abuse. For that reason, no one – not even the closest friend, relative or marriage partner – will be allowed access to those secrets. The victim will endeavour to carry on with life without facing up to what happened in earlier years. Here is a *'disassociation'* and a kind of defence mechanism used to block out hurtful memories of what happened to their bodies during the abuse. In some respects, this is partly successful but the victim suffers emotionally. For example, the victim may withdraw emotionally and physically from some relationships and feel repulsed by sex. There will also, and inevitably, be flashbacks resulting in mood swings, depression, guilt and possibly self-hatred.

Control

There is, however, a subtle twist here. In child abuse, the victim experiences a loss of control when his/her wishes and protests are ignored by the abuser. The latter usually threatens and frightens a child into secrecy which further compounds the problem. Victims feel 'dirty', guilty and afraid, even though they may not have been in a position to prevent the abuse occurring. In later years, if the victim marries without first receiving appropriate counselling, then she may become the abuser in the marital relationship, exercising **total control** over all aspects of the relationship, including sex. Intimacy may be declined and irrational behavioural attitudes of control exercised towards the marriage partner. The child victim of sexual abuse now becomes the abuser. In this story, the husband, a pastor, unknowingly at first, became the victim.

Challenge

Help is available for abuse victims, including those sexually abused in childhood. Considerable healing is possible with the appropriate help, enabling victims to move forward confidently and enjoy a happy marital relationship. It is against this background, that Dan's story of domestic abuse needs to be understood.

- There is also the stark warning to couples considering marriage for them to be completely open with one another and to be willing to seek counselling if any form of abuse has been suffered by one or both partners in earlier years.

- Here is an aspect which church leaders may want to introduce into marriage preparation classes as a possible preventative measure for addressing such unhappiness and possible domestic abuse in the future.

We turn in the next chapter to consider the impact which domestic abuse can have on children in the family who may witness it, often over a significant period of time. They tend to be forgotten and neglected.

ACTION POINTS

1. Identify examples of 'control' and 'abuse' in Dan's story.

2. Specify ways in which you think the church elders ought to have handled Dan's marital and abuse problem.

9. Children are Victims too!

Consider the following facts regarding children who witness domestic abuse in their homes:

- 20 per cent of children in the U.K. have been exposed to domestic abuse.
- Domestic violence is a factor in over a half of all serious case reviews of children.
- 130,000 children live in households with high risk domestic abuse.
- In 90 per cent of domestic abuse/violence incidents in family households, children were in the same, or the next room.
- In Scotland, one study found that one in two children who experienced domestic abuse had physically intervened to protect their mother during an attack.
- Too often children are threatened not to tell anyone about the abuse they witness in the family. They may too be compelled by the abuser to participate in the abuse.
- 62 per cent of the children in households where domestic abuse occurs, are also directly harmed in various ways by the abuse.
- 75 per cent of children on the 'at risk' register live in families where domestic abuse occurs.

- Children exposed to domestic abuse are more likely to have behavioural and emotional problems.
- Two thirds of the residents in the network of refuges in England and Wales are children. They make up some of the most vulnerable children in the country.
- Children witnessing domestic abuse is now legally regarded as child abuse.
- While the effects of domestic abuse on children can last into adulthood, it is NOT true that these children will inevitably become a perpetrator or a victim of abuse later in their lives.
- Some children and young people fear their own emotions like anger and can have difficulties in establishing and maintaining good relationships as adults.
- Domestic violence survivor and campaigner Rachel Williams was chosen as the new ambassador for Welsh Women's Aid. Shot by her former husband at a hair salon, Rachel was eager to help children brought up in abusive households to see that it is not normal. Rachel feels deeply concerned for such children especially as her sixteen-year-old son, Jack, committed suicide after his father tried to kill her. 'We need to do more', she emphasised, 'to help these children.'[1]

Children who witness domestic abuse in their families may themselves become aggressive, express anti-social behaviour, suffer depression/anxiety and under-perform in school. If a child becomes withdrawn, behaves out of character or is anxious and clingy, then these may be important indicators that the child is struggling to cope with the impact of domestic

---

1   *Western Mail*, 'Children's Champion in domestic abuse battle', Alicia Melville-Smith, (Saturday June 20, 2015), p. 18.

abuse. More serious indicators can be obsessive behaviour, nightmares, self-harm and suicidal thoughts.[2]

In the rest of this chapter, Miriam provides a personal account of the domestic abuse she witnessed in her family and its impact on her life. While circumstances vary, her story is representative of the deeply disturbing effect that domestic abuse has on children in the home. Their plight needs to be taken seriously in the context of pastoral care.

MY STORY: MIRIAM

My dad was always there – strong and protective of us as a family, and fixing things when needed. He was respected as a minister in a growing church; his ministry was appreciated locally and wider afield. I was proud that Dad was never at home in the evenings but always attending a meeting or visiting church members. He was so busy; cherished by his church but put on a pedestal as a model pastor.

The change was insidious and developed more in our family as I started senior school. This story of domestic abuse is entangled in a story of family breakdown with the abuse becoming more prevalent as the marriage between my parents disintegrated. My father became angry with his lot and his desire to get out of it took over.

The family set-up was a traditional one – my father was the bread-winner and my mother cared for the family, though mum worked sometimes when family finances required it. It was only after I reached adulthood that I learnt more about my father's controlling behaviour of her. Mum was respected as the minister's wife, but she had no close friends for my father alienated her from the church congregation and she was too afraid to have friends outside. He was the controlling

---

2   See for example *Effects of Domestic Violence on Children,* Ronald E. Sharp, William Gladden Foundation, 2014. This 'brief e-book about the effects of domestic violence on children is easy-to-read and to understand'. It is written for parents, guardians and family members as well as teachers and school staff. The book has limited value for the U.K..

factor in the house. Although we loved him, we were scared of him, even before the violence began. We knew it was his agreement we required for anything we wanted to do – there was no point asking Mam.

When my siblings first told me our father was 'having an affair' I thought it was laughable. But the 'other woman' was a member of the congregation. No one outside our small family unit knew – it started off as just quarrelling between my parents witnessed by us children from the back of the car. They tried to hide it from us, but soon it could not be hidden. My mum struggled to keep the family afloat whilst trying to save her marriage. Dad continued his affair, maintaining his public image as a minister.

My mum stayed in the situation to try to save her family life until I was in my mid-teens, but my teenage years were extremely lonely and insular. For the majority of this time, my siblings were in university and dealt with the family breakdown in their own ways. I dealt with the emotional chaos around me by closing down, seeking strength from within myself. My Mum was increasingly losing weight because of the strain she was under. My father prowled the house as we both tried to stay out of his way – until he roared at something which caused him displeasure. The atmosphere at home was one of fear. Mum and myself were like small mice scurrying round near the skirting boards. I would move around the house quickly, from one room to another trying to be invisible. I buried myself in television programmes or in my bedroom, listening to music. I often lay lonely on my bed listening to the emotional cries and chaos outside my bedroom. I was desperate for the situation to improve but also worried my parents may separate. Could I endure the emotional and physical turmoil or the embarrassment in school and in church? It was unthinkable. On occasions I saw bruises and grazes on mum's arms and legs which she tried to hide. The next Sunday we would be back in our usual church seat, the minister's wife and child, smiling and apparently gaining spiritual succour from the pulpit. My father would smile at his congregation, put his hand on my shoulder as I stood with him whilst he shook hands at the church door. But it was the same hand I also saw on my mother's shoulder and around my mother's throat, which my father grabbed and squeezed until she fell down on the floor in pain and exhaustion.

My first recollection of my father's physical anger was seeing him and mum quarrelling in their bedroom, my mother telling me tearfully that my father intended to leave. My father forced mum's arm up behind her back until she was crying in pain. He pushed her to her chest and she was thrown across their double bed until she nearly fell off the other side. I fell on my knees, threw my arms around his legs and pleaded with him not to leave us. He carried on walking out of the bedroom, dragging me with him, trying to push me aside and kick me away, telling me not to be silly – he had to leave. He couldn't cope living there with us. He claimed my mother was telling lies about him and he would not tolerate it.

Another time, I saw him pushing my mother backwards over the bannister of our upstairs landing, as if to throw her over and down the stairwell. I am told that I returned to my bedroom to cry alone through the night. My father would not allow my mum to comfort me, and I went to school the following day with swollen red eyes, with no words or hugs of comfort, no breakfast. However, when my class teacher asked me about my tears and the change she had noticed in my demeanour over months, the floodgates opened and I told her everything. Thankfully she insisted I share my problems with my closest school friend – the only two people I confided in for those teenage years. This friend was a huge help. Emotional abuse is real but I felt I had no emotional support from within the home during those years - I felt that all decisions that I made were my own. The reality may have been different. Witnessing such violence between parents at close quarters is emotionally harmful but one incident in particular stands out for me concerning the emotional pressure I felt under.

I was a reserved teenager and spending a lonely November evening hidden away in the lounge amidst the quarrelling. Then I saw my mother outside the French window of the lounge, in the darkness knocking frantically for me to let her into the lounge. My father had locked her out of the house. As I ran to let her in, my father burst into the room, dragging me away from the door and forbad me to open it. We spent ten minutes in a triangle of agony – my mother crying and beseeching outside for me to let her in; my father stood in the doorway, just outside of my mother's view, his finger pointing at me, towering over me, telling me I should not open the door. My eyes tried to convey to my mother how much I would love to open the door. When my father walked away, I ventured toward the French window to open it for her. He returned to prevent me again. She asked me to pass out a cardigan or scarf or something for her – he would not let me. I was grateful when my mother eventually walked away into the darkness. She walked around the locality in her slippers and dress in the cold. Returning to the house an hour later, she saw my father drive away to the prayer meeting, she knew I would let her in. There were many similar incidents but this one sticks in my mind. I carry the feelings of guilt of having let my mother down on this, and other occasions. I have a very close relationship with my mother still – but guilt is one of the foundation stones on which it is built.

The worst incident by far occurred after this, when I learnt the lesson of how cold and harsh this man could be. Sundays were always the worst of days as this meant attending church with my father preaching, whilst the woman with whom he was having his 'affair' was also in the congregation. The only people in the building who knew of this were mum and myself. On this particular morning, my mother was taken home ill before the service but throughout the service my chest and throat ached with hatred toward my father for his behaviour at home, anger toward the church for revering him and all this complicated by my love for him as my dad.

We were the last to leave the service and in walking to the car, my father said: 'Your mother is very ill. She is ill in the head. She has taken some pills and you should prepare yourself that she may not live much longer.' I remember my eyes stinging as the tears started to well. I found it hard to breathe. This was what it was like to face your mother dying, I thought. He showed no trace of emotion either for her or for me. I sensed he did not care and there was an aura of excitement about him. He encouraged me to go and see my mum in bed. She was pale and smiled as I walked in. Thankfully, her doctor had been called and was with her. Years later, I learned that mum had taken an overdose of medication in an attempt at suicide and my father had stood over her taunting her to take it. She had then driven herself to church but collapsed before the service began. Someone kindly took her home and telephoned her doctor. My father's questioning of my mother's health chilled the doctor for dad appeared to not want his wife to recover.

I also remember my father's violence toward my older siblings and there were dreadful instances. I don't know why he did not lift a hand against me – perhaps because I was younger, or because I tried to stay out of his way and did not try to confront him about his behaviour until much later, when I was safely out of his house. I felt helpless to do anything.

His control over us as children, often through threats, sometimes violence, went on for years – even into our young adulthood. Christmas was always a time of stress and tears during these years; the atmosphere was tense. My father had managed, following his separation, to maintain the pastorate of his church, through the lies he spread about my mum and the misguided support he received from members and local evangelicals. Dad tried to ensure for example that as children we were fully supportive of him and distrusting of mum. This he did through ensuring we were always at church listening to him preach, which meant my weekends were spent with him and every Christmas Day too – despite longing to be with my mother. It would be easy to criticise us but he controlled us through years of apparent love interspersed with anger, threats, violence and overt discipline even when we left home. As my parents' marriage difficulties became known to church officers, my father continued controlling, lying and being powerful and credible to the end. Many believed him. When I left for university, he married the woman whom my mother had identified years previously. He never apologised or repented.

1. The effect on me: as a child within the home

God's hand was on me throughout this awful time, though no one pastored me during these years. My father was not a pastor to me. As I grew older, my love and pride in him grew into emotions more of fear, at times terror, disdain then hatred. No-one in the church tried to pastor me either – a real failure. I understand they did not know how to deal with my mum and her hurt or myself and my siblings. My mother was often hurt by the insensitivity, lack of belief and understanding of Christians but also by the lies that spread through church circles about her – started by my father.

As children we seemed to have been forgotten in a sea of chaos. I felt awash in an abyss where no one seemed to care for me – my mother was dealing with her own hurt and was emotionally helpless to deal with mine. I was unable to confide in my closest friend at church as her parents had supported my father. The level at which my father appeared to care about me as compared to how much he cared for the appearance of having my support, has never left me.

After my parents' separation – even though the violence between them had stopped – I still felt tormented in my father's company and took on my mother's role of seeking out evidence of his continuing adulterous relationship. I felt in an emotional and spiritual wilderness – completely lost. I recall vividly one occasion looking at my father as he prepared food for us both. A kitchen scissors on top of the fridge caught my attention and I was severely tempted by it but I was restrained and walked to the safety of my bedroom again. There were dark moments for me; the Lord seemed far away, although I knew I was a Christian, my faith felt nearly snuffed out. Whilst adults around me failed to minister to me, I experienced the sufficiency of the Lord's grace. Probably many people were praying for me and I read a chapter of my Bible every day. Strangely, although I spent weekends with my father, sometimes piano playing and singing hymns, made me feel closer to my mother who spent her weekends alone. These hymns, full of Scripture and of Christ, were a huge source of spiritual comfort and ministry to me. Looking back, I see how much I was helped by these means, through God's grace.

2. Effect on me as I left home

I have very few childhood memories that are not tainted by a sourness of my father's influence, although God blessed me with a generally positive outlook throughout my adolescence.

My philosophy was to endure the next few years until I left home for University. My siblings, mum and myself experienced a great deal of hatred and lies from Christians, including ministers, elders and those with influence in Christian circles. They chose only to believe my father but as children we knew what was happening at home and were entirely behind my mother, although controlled by my father.

In setting off for University, I longed for freedom, leaving church and to be with people who knew nothing of my family. God had other plans! On my first night, having walked with a school friend aimlessly around the pubs, I wandered back to the Student Hall of Residence straight into the Christian Union fresher's outreach event! I met and made firm friends with a young Christian who guided me to a welcoming church and supported me as I started to feel again the warmth of wanting to learn more about God. My steps that night were firmly in God's hands.

However, my faith continued to fluctuate and sometimes I rebelled against God yet he gave me people to guide me back to him at the exact times when I was running in the opposite direction! Whilst in University my father re-married and had to leave his church. He married the woman whom my mother had identified years ago as the cause of the marriage breakdown and many saw my mum had told the truth. I tried to maintain a relationship with my father but disliked him and we barely saw each other although a sense of duty ensured we remained in tortuous telephone contact.

Encountering domestic abuse alongside the breakdown of your parents' marriage is an extremely painful process. However, that this happened at the hands of a Minister of the Gospel affects one's Christian life. Coming to terms with my father's abusive controlling nature, his adultery, his continuing deceit and unwillingness to acknowledge, even a small part, the hurt that my family and I endured has plagued me emotionally and spiritually. Even as an adult, my father sought to control my actions; for example, he stopped his monthly financial support for my student days without giving me notice. He threatened to walk out of our wedding ceremony as he did not approve of our choice of speaker and carried this out after 'giving me away' and just before the sermon to make his point.

When I was heavily pregnant with our first child he told us we would have to reconsider our position on not forging a relationship with his wife. In these situations I dug my heels in to break his emotional control over me but the hurt continued. As my children grew and my father's health deteriorated, God showed me through the wise counsel of others that I should foster again my relationship with him. This was very painful as I also had to build a relationship with his wife so I could visit and take the children there. I am glad I did so. I built a different relationship with him to that of a father/daughter as I felt I had lost and mourned my 'father-figure' after his second marriage and our subsequent estrangement.

When my father became critically ill, this even meant on some occasions, staying overnight in his house where I had grown up, seen him abuse my mother and siblings. However, it did mean that one of my siblings and I were able to be at his bedside holding his hand and singing hymns to him as he passed away. I have no reason to believe he was remorseful for what he did to us, nor repentant. However, the Lord gave me strength in this difficult time to visit and care for him and I share this to show that some measure of forgiveness and re-building of relationships in these times can bring some healing for the victim or child-witness.

It may be difficult or impossible in many situations to rebuild a relationship with the perpetrator of domestic abuse. But in my circumstance, having some sort of resolution to my relationship with my father, allowed me to get on with my life, without allowing his actions to hurt me further. His actions were so detrimental to me spiritually that I consider this restoring of relationships as part of God's plan for my ultimate benefit.

3. Effect on me as a wife and mother

I have concerns that I have some of my father's personality traits and I have had to work hard analysing my actions as a wife/mother because of my upbringing. During our early quarrels in married life, I would often lose the battle of not using similar language with my husband to that which I had heard my father use with mum. I have been able to identify and analyse times when I would try to manipulate and have control in situations within our marriage. I had to work hard at modifying my behaviour and at seeking to fully understand the biblical model of marriage – though often failing to live by it. In raising and disciplining my children also, I have heard the echoes of my father in my own voice and have on one occasion especially, scared myself by losing my temper as I saw my father do.

Only after my father's death, have I felt completely free to talk about his abusive nature and am no longer trapped emotionally and psychologically by a kind of loyalty toward him whilst he was alive and a form of love toward the father I longed I had had during childhood.

Key words used by Miriam include:

'fear', 'terror', 'controlling', 'lies', 'helpless', 'guilt', 'stress', 'tormented', 'insidious', 'lonely', 'desperate' and 'dreadful'.

In the next chapters we begin to look in more detail at a pastoral response to domestic abuse.

ACTION POINTS

1. In which ways does Miriam's experience of domestic abuse as a child alert us to the suffering of children in such circumstances?

2. Trace Miriam's later struggle to overcome the influence on her life of her father's control.

PART THREE
RESPONDING TO
DOMESTIC ABUSE
PASTORALLY

10. Responding Pastorally: Guidelines

Christians, and especially church officers, need help in understanding domestic abuse in terms of its complexity, its massive impact on victims/children but also its implications for the future, including the safety and then restoration of the victims. Abusers too need help, if they are willing. There are no simplistic answers and each situation is distinctive although similar patterns of thinking, behaviour and response can be identified. In the light of what has been shared in earlier chapters, it is appropriate now to retrace our steps and enlarge on some of the facts which have already emerged.

A. HELP IN RECOGNISING AND RESPONDING TO DOMESTIC ABUSE

1. Silence

Nearly all victims of domestic abuse are afraid or embarrassed to tell anyone else, even relatives, about their situation. Often the abused has been threatened not to tell anyone about the abuse and one popular threat is to take the children away from the victim or even to threaten death. Victims can feel very frightened. For that reason, domestic abuse is 'shrouded in silence'; it is a 'secret crime' committed within the privacy of the home and far from the gaze of others. For Rita, she did not tell anyone because of feelings of shame coupled with the thought that no one would believe her story. And then there was the nagging fear that if she told someone, perhaps her domestic situation would get even worse. Sometimes relatives may suspect there is a problem but deny that the abuse exists or they may feel helpless to intervene. In the experience of Louise whose story was told earlier, she believed that in being married she must stoically accept all that happened in her marriage and not complain to her parents or peers about the abuse. The fact is that, whatever the reason, secrecy can be maintained for a considerable length of time by victims with no one suspecting the abuse.

2. Signs

Because of the secrecy involved in cases of domestic abuse, a church may mistakenly assume there are no such problems within its fellowship. However, if a church has a fair number of people attending services then it is reasonable to assume that one person at least will be experiencing abuse. If the church is large then there are likely to be several victims of domestic abuse amongst its members and adherents. The question arises, if the abuse is hidden, are there signs to look out for which may suggest a person is a victim of domestic abuse? The following signs may at least indicate difficulties in a marriage but they may also point to domestic abuse. These signs, therefore, are not infallible, so the importance of a pastor and church elders knowing their people well is extremely relevant at this point.

If the wife, for example, is never seen apart from her husband or never speaks to another person without the husband hearing the conversation then one may wonder what is happening. The victim may not have friends or makes excuses for not meeting them. Attending church meetings may become infrequent and the victim is isolated increasingly from the church community or relatives.

Another indicator may be that the wife is unwilling to speak for herself in company because her husband takes control of the conversation, answering questions on her behalf. Her partner appears to be controlling her and may even insult or disparage her in front of others.

Sometimes their home is 'off-bounds' to friends, even a pastor, and no one is welcomed, even if they call. The abuser may become more unsociable and rude with her family and make her more dependent on him financially. The children too can be unruly and moody in school and in church; they may also cling to their mother when outside the home, refusing to leave her. These factors can at least alert church leaders that something wrong may be taking place within the home.

To put it bluntly, however, it can be difficult to identify a person suffering domestic abuse. Who would have suspected that Dan was a victim? After all, he was the successful pastor of a large Bible-believing church. And from the outside, it seemed to be a very happy marriage. Or who suspected that Charlotte was being abused by her pastor-husband? He was a preacher widely respected. What about Louise who quietly suffered abuse in marriage for fifteen years without sharing with anyone in her family or church? Mary too kept the dark secret of domestic abuse to herself for years with no one in church suspecting anything was wrong. For that reason, we must not be hard on church officers for not spotting domestic abuse in their church communities. If there are no broken bones or visible bruises or black eyes for them to see, then normally one assumes an individual has no problem with abuse. If it is emotional, psychological, financial, sexual or even spiritual abuse which is suffered then again, the church may not be able to identify it easily. It is hidden. This highlights the fact that it is impossible for church leaders to be privy to what happens privately between a husband and wife. And this, I repeat, is a further challenge for pastors and church elders to observe carefully and build healthy relationships with those in the church family.

3. Phases in abuse

In Christian marriages where domestic abuse occurs, the first few months of marriage may be enjoyable with few, if any, early signs of abuse emerging. Louise, for example, reports that the early months of marriage were 'good initially. I was happy ... we seemed to get on ok'. Others like Rita, Charlotte and Dan can provide a similar story. Gradually, however, the relationship changes and is characterised by increasing tension, disagreement, shouting, threats and accusations, even violence. For Charlotte the physical abuse came later while for Louise the abuse was almost wholly manipulative and psychological. For Rita the physical abuse emerged earlier alongside spiritual and psychological abuse. This continued until eventual separation and divorce took place, but for her, even afterwards, the spiritual abuse remained dominant alongside the emotional and psychological abuse. For others, physical abuse reaches a point where the victim's life is in danger and to urge the woman to return to such an abusive husband would be wrong. If there is an absence of physical violence and even if verbal and emotional abuse are manageable, the 'control' level can yet be overwhelming. Church officers need to be aware of different patterns in domestic abuse when seeking to help a victim. The 'control' aspect is in no way confined to physical abuse.

4. Caution

Caution is necessary on the part of anyone caring pastorally for abuse victims. There is no quick-fix because a domestic abuse victim needs time and patience from anyone seeking to help. The trust of the victim also needs to be gained as well as an awareness of the nature and extent of the abuse. Is the victim and her children's lives in danger? Pastoral advice can sometimes be unwise and endanger the victim's life. Finding a balance between caution and action requires much prayer, love and wisdom. For example, it is necessary to listen carefully to the victim. To hear the full story may require several sessions over days or months as the initial disclosure will only be the tip of an iceberg. Perhaps there is much more one needs to hear before safely concluding whether the relationship is abusive or not. Victims are crying out for pastors and others to listen to them. While listening to the victim however, the pastor may feel out of his depth and unable to advise. One lady who has suffered domestic abuse herself, offers the following advice:

> *'It's vital that pastors recognise and acknowledge their limitations. Leaders who are uncertain about what to do (and willing to be upfront about it!), are less likely to give potentially dangerous advice and more likely to seek advice from others. I remember in my case that Pastor admitted to being out of his depth, but he was willing to provide a safe place when needed without feeling he had to find solutions or tell me what to do. Perhaps there needs to be a general change in churches' expectations that leaders should always have the answers, and that leaders would be humble in recognising that they can get it wrong too.'* [1]

Over the years, pastors in England and Wales have shared with me their struggles in coping with cases of domestic abuse in their churches. Their honesty, caution and humility were refreshing; they needed advice and support.

---

1   Email correspondence, June 2016.

5. An appeal

From among Christian survivors of domestic abuse, there are regular voices making their appeal to churches; it is a reasonable appeal. One aspect of this appeal is for churches to admit that domestic abuse takes place in marriages both for Christians and unbelievers. This must be emphasised for domestic abuse exists in varying degrees and forms within some Christian marriages. Again, they ask that we do not judge or criticise victims but listen to their story carefully and believe them. They want to be believed and receive support from the pastor and other church leaders. Too often they are all alone, so to be accepted, then believed by a pastor, can make an enormous difference to them. Another appeal is for pastors in their preaching to mention occasionally such abuse while emphasising the duty of husbands to love their wives. For too many victims, the church is silent on the subject.

Another interesting aspect of their appeal is for church leaders to be fair in considering their appeal for help. On occasions, the abuser may be prominent and popular in a church with the result that the victim's story is rejected as not being credible. Dan's experience where the church elders only listened to the abuser is salutary; they did not listen to both parties and that is grossly unfair. The abuse is swept under the carpet and the victim loses his reputation as well as the friendships he valued so much in the church.

6. Confidentiality

A further aspect of the appeal is for confidentiality. Amongst the reasons why a victim may not approach a pastor or someone else in the church for help is the question: can I trust 'X' and will he maintain strict confidentiality if I tell him about my situation? That is a genuine fear. Too often confidentiality is lacking in Christian circles and individuals are deeply hurt when they discover that their personal problems have been shared with others without permission. On their behalf, I appeal for confidentiality in counselling.

However, there may be an exception in cases of abuse. A victim can be reassured of confidentiality but told that it may be necessary to pursue the matter further. This may be in order to follow child protection procedures or, if the victim is in considerable danger, then the Police and Women's Aid. A refuge may need to be consulted. Again, the victim needs to be informed of this course of action and understand why it is being taken. Charlotte shared earlier how grateful she felt that the one person in church who eventually knew about the abuse she suffered, did not 'push' her but was prepared to help at her pace when she was ready. He maintained strict confidentiality and did not even share with his wife. This is what victims want. They desire confidentiality and the opportunity to approve any action which a pastor or counsellor may wish to take. What if the victim refuses permission to report the abuse? You cannot force the victim to agree to any action or referral but it is important to keep the lines of communication open and to meet with the victim when necessary or when requested. Brief notes of your meetings and joint decisions taken can be important in the future.

7. Earlier?

One of the questions arising when pastoring victims of domestic abuse, is: why do victims remain in an abusive marriage relationship for a long period, often for ten, fifteen or more years? Some answers have already been hinted at in the stories related by victims who suffered abuse for years. Why did they not raise an alarm earlier?

One victim explains that if she had shared the problems and distress of the early years then the abuse would as a consequence have reached a new level. A further factor in her thinking was disloyalty to the husband and a failure in her duties and role as a wife. Marriage had been a serious commitment she had entered into freely and prayerfully. In marrying the man who became her husband, she had resolved to suffer the consequences if things went wrong. Marriage was 'for better or for worse'! And there was the hope that the marriage may improve.

Another reason for not pulling out of the marriage earlier was her desire for parents, peers and friends to become Christians. Separating from her husband at an earlier stage may have pushed them further away from the Christian faith. Again, she had young children who needed a father figure and as mother she needed his practical support. Related to this was the fear her husband might take the children away from her, if she left. That was a very real fear. Underlying some of these reasons was a conviction that marriage was for life and that divorce was permissible only on the grounds of adultery. There was no way out, she reasoned.

Some or all of these reasons resonate with other victims of domestic abuse. Of course, other reasons can be added, but one further reason deserves a mention. That is the feeling of helplessness and dependence which a wife can feel after years of 'control' by her husband so that decision-making is extremely difficult. And a decision to leave a husband on whom she depends seems impossible. Pastorally, these reasons may help us understand why some victims are reluctant to leave the abuser.

8. Perception of a victim

One victim seeking to help other women suffering domestic abuse shared the following helpful advice:

Don't expect victims to conform to one's perception of a victim. This woman can appear confident and direct, and some incidents she tells me about suggest she is able to stand up for herself. This could lead someone ... to think both partners are responsible for the problems. Added to this is the 'tip of the iceberg' problem where you only get small hints of what is actually going on ... it has taken a huge amount of time: picking up on the hints ... listening to what she wants to tell me ... there is a lot to be said for taking time and reserving judgement if one isn't sure whether the relationship is actually abusive.[2]

9) Forgiveness?

Some survivors of domestic abuse struggle with the question of forgiveness. Should they forgive their abuser, and even if he/she is unrepentant? This is a complex issue and Christians vary in giving one of two answers – answers they believe are in line with Bible teaching. A helpful summary of these two different responses is provided by Eric E. Wright in his book, *Revolutionary Forgiveness.*[3] It is beyond the scope of this book to pursue the subject in detail but the following guidelines may be helpful:

- Forgiveness is not a top priority in urgent and dangerous relationships. Issues such as the safety of the survivor and the children, practical provision for their needs, pastoral support in terms of counselling and care assume greater urgency and priority.
- Forgiveness should not be approached from one side alone, that is the side of the victim because forgiveness is a *'relational event'.*[4] There is a tendency to treat forgiveness as an isolated event, unrelated to the whole pattern and

---

2   E-mail correspondence 10/6/2016.

3   Darlington, England, Evangelical Press, 2002, pp. 207-225.

4   *Responding to Domestic Abuse: Guidelines*, p. 20.

history of the relationship; this kind of approach ought to be avoided.

- Forgiveness as a positive response by the survivor, does not side-line issues of justice and the accountability of the abuser. Forgiveness and justice are not mutually exclusive; it is possible for the abuser to be helped and restrained by the law and professional agencies yet for the survivor to extend forgiveness without seeking reconciliation.

- Forgiveness can be helpful to some survivors, particularly in recognising that her/his reactions in abusive situations were not always God-honouring, although not the cause for abuse. The survivor's sense of guilt in recalling sinful responses to the abuse can become a burden for some individuals.

Miriam, who suffered as a child from witnessing domestic abuse in her family, was able to 'show a measure of forgiveness' to her abusive father. For her, this provided 'some sort of resolution' but also 'allowed me to get on with my life', she writes. This was also a help in 'not getting hurt further by his actions'.

At this point, **Louise's** experience is helpful and confirmatory in highlighting the positive and negative aspects of the survivor taking an initiative to forgive, apart from repentance on the part of the perpetrator. Leading up to separation from her husband, Louise acknowledges that 'my thoughts were full of all the negative things about my marriage... It felt like an obsession, and painful, negative bitter feelings consumed many of my thoughts... I became fed up with feeling hurt... I wanted to let go of those feelings.' What stopped her from doing so? 'I was worried that if I stopped being angry, and forgave him, I would want to return to my marriage... but the way I felt about my husband felt sinful…'.[5] And then what? Louise felt she ought to deal with her feelings of bitterness and 'forgiveness felt like the right thing to do before God as well as the best thing for me to do… to move forward in my life…' She spoke to her husband 'and said sorry for all the things I had done wrong. I told him that I had forgiven him for the husband he had been.'

What has this meant for Louise? One important factor in forgiving her ex-husband is that she 'no longer felt any anger towards him', although strongly disapproving of the abuse he inflicted on her. This sense of relief from guilt also meant more peace of mind in complying with the Bible's teaching on 'walking in love', involving the absence of bitterness and anger (Eph. 4:26,30-32, 5:1-2). Her initiative in seeking forgiveness was clearly an expression of personal repentance, her desire to please the Lord, to be rid of guilt and not to be obsessed with negative, bitter thoughts.

Her action in seeking forgiveness from her abuser, did not condone the way she had been abused over the years. There are subtle dangers here, however, for in being rid of her anger she may feel tempted to return to the abusive relationship. She writes: 'I still knew that it was better for me to live separately from him. I knew that it was better for my children, and that when I was with him his controlling behaviour had led to me losing my sense of identity and diminished me as a person. While that was true, from this point onwards, I have swung between feelings of wanting to return to him, and reasoning with myself that I must not…' Louise, and others like her, need to recognise that forgiveness does not entail mediation or reconciliation.

This is an area which requires more attention in the church's teaching and pastoral work.

---

5   E-mail 2-6-2018.

10. The abuser

Pastorally, the abuser must not be forgotten. They need help but their responses vary considerably. There are some success stories but in my pastoral experience, I cannot point to one abuser who has genuinely repented. I have found that they can be extremely charming and persuasive in explaining /defending, their abusive behaviour. Like other pastoral workers, I have often felt out of my depth in addressing their needs. Why not then refer a perpetrator to a qualified counsellor and use helpful resources and agencies, if the person is willing? Here is one useful resource I like: *Information for men who are concerned about their behaviour towards their partner.* This is available from *info@respectphoneline.org.uk.*[6] This resource describes various forms of abuse together with its impact on women and children. Men are then offered advice on how to stop their abusive behaviour. A confidential helpline is available as well as information on a prevention programme. There is also a similar resource for heterosexual women who want to understand more about their violence and abuse towards their partner.

B. UNDERSTANDING ASPECTS OF DOMESTIC ABUSE

1. Financial abuse

One lady who is in touch with wives being abused by their husbands informs me: *'Interestingly, for all the people I have spoken to so far, money is a major issue – debt, unwise/reckless/profligate spending, depriving women of money or insisting that women are responsible for earning sufficient to sustain the household when the man keeps every penny they earn to spend on themselves. I confess I*

---

6   Other useful websites include: www.hiddenhurt.co.uk/;
     www.freedomprogramme.co.uk/; the BBC website HITTING HOME.

was surprised at the strength and predominance of this common thread among the women I have spoken to.'[7]

Financial abuse can easily be ignored but it is one way in which abusers exercise control over partners and make them more dependent. Charlotte found this to be a significant way in which her husband controlled her. Dan's wife too exercised 'almost complete control' and monitored critically his spending, even for a coffee on his journey home. Another victim of domestic abuse who helps abused women warns us: '…even where there is no physical abuse, the verbal/emotional abuse can seem comparatively mild… but the level of control can be extreme. Refusing access to money is controlling in itself; it also disempowers the "victim", so that she is less likely to believe she can "escape" or provide for herself (or her children). Lack of money makes it harder to access legal advice and, in this case… she is seldom allowed to leave the home alone …'[8] This financial abuse meant that this woman on one occasion, '"stole" some money to buy food and cups of coffee'. She urges us neither to condone or be judgemental; '…it is perhaps more helpful to use this behaviour as an indicator of how extreme the situation is. We are called to be compassionate …' In these and other situations, money becomes a weapon for controlling and isolating a partner – it is a powerful weapon.

2. Emotional abuse
Emotional abuse is not easily detected yet it is common both in society and in churches. This form of abuse 'represents an oppressive and insidious process that strikes deeply at the hearts of its victims'. It is 'dehumanizing', leaving its victims

---

7   Email correspondence: 'G', 7 June 2016.

8   E-mail correspondence, 10 June, 2016.

'feeling confused, vulnerable, trapped, and worthless.'[9] The abuser is desperate to achieve control for a variety of reasons including his/her own feelings of inadequacy and insecurity. There is usually too for Christians a misguided interpretation of biblical teaching concerning the wife's duty to 'submit' to the husband; he may also have a deep-seated fear of losing his wife. The abuser may then intimidate, use verbal abuse, frighten and criticise but also lie and deceive. It is the constant pressure and use of these factors which add to the pain and anguish of emotional abuse. The wife feels trapped, is deprived of self-confidence and any sense of hope regarding the future. Her feelings are those of complete hopelessness and despair. Indicators of an emotionally abused wife may be low self-esteem and self-hatred though appearing in public outwardly confident. Feelings of guilt are often deep, sometimes associated with abuse, though not necessarily. What needs to be appreciated is the subtle and complex nature of emotional abuse which makes the victim feel utterly worthless.

3. Psychological abuse

This is obviously related but it is difficult to distinguish it from emotional abuse. Examples of psychological abuse were given in chapter four. Perhaps emotional abuse majors more on the impact of abuse on the victim while psychological abuse also draws attention to the subtle and deliberate schemes of the abuser to distress and frighten the victim. This is achieved in different ways, partly through using mind-games and frightening the victim by means of multiple threats which can involve the children and other close relatives. The fearful anticipation of further abuse only increases the tension and anxiety which in turn gives satisfaction to the abuser.

---

9   'The Silent Killer of Christian Marriages', Amy Wildman White, from Catherine C
     Kroeger & James R. Beck, eds, *Healing the Hurting*, (Baker, 1998).

4) Spiritual abuse

Spiritual abuse is rarely spoken about in churches but it exists in subtle forms in church life. Within the context of marriage, the abuser may accuse his wife of being a child of the devil; as such she could not be loved by God. Constant criticisms and accusations concerning the victim's behaviour, sins and alleged failures serve to undermine the person's assurance of salvation, resulting in feelings of desperation and guilt. This aspect of domestic abuse needs to be opened up further by asking basic questions:

Q: What is spiritual abuse?[10]

A: *It is an expression of psychological and emotional abuse but within a religious context. Often it means that individuals are 'being controlled, coerced and pressurised within churches and places of worship',[11] but also in some Christian homes. The term 'spiritual abuse' began to be employed approximately twenty years ago but it is often misunderstood.*

Q: What does spiritual abuse look like?

A: *The Churches Child Pastoral Advisory Service (CCPAS) uses the acronym **BADIS** to set out helpfully some of its key features:*

Blame: unable to give an opinion or raise issues without being threatened and blamed.

---

10   See L.R.Oakley & K.S. Kinmond *Breaking the silence on spiritual abuse*, (Palgrave McMillan,2013), p. 21: 'Spiritual abuse is coercion and control of one individual by another in a spiritual context. The target experiences ...a deeply emotional personal attack' and 'may include manipulation and exploitation, enforced accountability, censorship of decision making, requirements for secrecy and silence, pressure to conform, misuse of scripture or the pulpit to control behaviour, requirement of obedience to the abuser, the suggestion that the abuser has a "divine" position isolation from others, especially those external to the abusive context.'

11   *Help ... I want to understand spiritual abuse:* Churches Child Pastoral Advisory Service (CCPAS), January 2018, p. 2.

Accountability in which one is often forced or coerced to share personal details.

Damage is 'a key feature in the individual's experience occurring through manipulation, fear and shame they may also be expected to be extremely committed to the place of worship... People often feel scared of the consequences of not conforming. They may also feel shame ... experience acceptance, followed by rejection, as a way of controlling their behaviour'.

Inability to work with others and unable to accept alternative opinions. There is often absence of team decision-making.

Scripture is often used out of context and misapplied in order to pressurise individuals to behave in a specific way and can be very difficult to cope with and argue against.

Q: Who are the abusers?

A: *Literally, anyone! Husbands or wives, church leaders, youth and children's workers, individual members. But remember also that church leaders can be abused spiritually by others in a church. A wife too can be as abusive in this respect as a husband.*

Q: How helpful is it to use the term 'spiritual abuse'?

A: *Victims who are Christians are often aware of the scripture being misused against them to 'control' and compel them to obey and remain submissive. Those who study the subject argue that basically it is all about power and exercising control over an individual, family or church whether the context is religious or not. For that reason, they are reluctant to employ the term 'spiritual abuse' and prefer to understand it under psychological and emotional abuse. Krish Kandiah suggests that whether in marriage, the church, the Police, the British Army, football or the film industry and the 'celebrity' world, 'fundamentally it comes down to the* *all-too-common abuse of power'.[12] Church leaders especially need to give careful consideration to this complex area of spiritual abuse in marriage but also in all areas of church life. Do we recognise spiritual abuse where it occurs within our churches and are any church leaders guilty of misusing their position and authority? This is an urgent matter for churches because for the first time the Church of England formally found one of its clergy guilty of 'spiritual abuse'. The 10 bishops disciplinary tribunal decided that Timothy Davis, vicar of a large evangelical parish church in the Oxfordshire town of Abingdon was guilty of 'conduct unbecoming to the office and work of a clerk of holy orders through the abuse of spiritual power and authority'.[13] The clergyman was guilty of 'intense mentoring' of a teenage boy and seeking to 'control' his life and relationships 'by use of admonition, Scripture, prayer...' How careful are we in our own churches? CCPAS found that in an on-line survey of over 1,500 churchgoers, two-thirds claimed they had personally experienced spiritual abuse in varied ways. Church members and young people as well as children and the elderly can be vulnerable so this whole area of spiritual abuse needs to be addressed with sensitive, relevant Bible teaching.*

In the next chapter we will consider suggestions and guidelines for responding pastorally to domestic abuse.

ACTION POINTS:

1. Do I respect the reasons given by victims of abuse for remaining silent?

2. How important is forgiveness in abusive relationships?

3. Do others know they can trust you to keep their problem confidential?

4. Could there be examples of 'spiritual abuse' in your church?

---

12   *Does the Church's First Spiritual Abuse Verdict Give Critics a New Weapon?* Krish Kandiah, *Christianity Today*, 12 January 2018.

13   *Christianity Today*, 12 January 2018.

11. Responding Pastorally: Suggestions

I remember the occasion and the date well. It was only a few months ago. The location was our home. My wife and I were sitting in the lounge sharing with a dear Christian lady, now a single mum, who had suffered domestic abuse for several years. It was not the first time for her to be in our home as we had been available for her over a long period and knew the dreadful and merciless abuse she had suffered and which her children had witnessed. Although divorced, she nevertheless continued to suffer psychological and financial abuse from a man who claimed to be a Christian. This occasion was different. I wanted to ply her with questions in an attempt to appreciate pastorally what could have been done, or done better, by her church and what could have been done at an earlier stage to help her. Although I knew her well and respected her as a child of God, I wanted to hear again from her the story of abuse and how she struggled but also what would have helped her in the varied aspects of her complex situation.

We started at the very beginning. There were tears, of course, but also a sense of the Lord being with us. This young mother had been given so much grace and strength in her problems to trust and honour the Lord. She had been upheld and kept by the Lord in the most desperate times. In listening to her story, we were compelled to admire the grace of God in her life.

This chapter is initially about this meeting and I am drawing on my extensive notes to describe what this lady shared. My main interest is pastoral, in seeking to understand what she went through, to appreciate her own perspective but also how a church, as well as individual believers, could have been more available and supportive for her. She is being given a different name and, in this chapter, I refer to her as Elen. Following Elen, Louise, Isabella and Vera also offer suggestions for improving pastoral care for those experiencing domestic abuse

PART A: DOMESTIC ABUSE VICTIMS – THEIR SUGGESTIONS FOR PASTORAL CARE

1. Elen

Q: Remind us of the extent of the domestic abuse you suffered.

A: *It was the whole range of physical, psychological, verbal, emotional, financial as well as spiritual abuse. All possible aspects of abuse were there all the time and I did not know what he would do next to abuse and harm me. I was afraid of him. He showed no mercy.*

Q: The children also witnessed the abuse. Is that correct?

A: *Yes. The older children witnessed more physical violence and the younger felt more the impact of the psychological, emotional and financial abuse. The children were often embarrassed then used as tools to get at me. But I endeavoured to retain as happy a family life as possible, and especially after we separated.*

Q: How did you seek to help the children in this situation?

A: *It was very difficult. I did the basic things in loving and caring for them. They were a priority. They were confused and hurt; their frustration and anger would often be redirected towards myself. We*

talked about it together and shared but I also led family worship where we would pray and talk about some of the matters affecting us. There were individuals who helped sometimes with school homework and other matters but, basically I felt I was on my own. I gave the children priority yet would have appreciated more help with others getting alongside them. I gave the children all the love I could.

Q: Like other victims, it was a long time before you shared your problem and sought pastoral help. Why was that?

A: *There was a deep sense of shame on my part that this was happening. And the shame is hard to describe. I also felt that no one would believe me but as well I feared that the situation would get worse if I asked for help. I was confused and did not know what to do.*

Q: What has been the impact of psychological abuse on you?

A: *Massive! My husband played mind games with me for years in twisting Scripture, accusing me incessantly and misinterpreting what I said and did. I began to believe what he told me about being ugly, stupid and good for nothing. He also told me that I was a wretched sinner, God could not love me and that I was a child of the devil. I began to feel numb and had no emotions; I was forgetting that God really loved me in Christ. Fear was very real too which meant I was not always thinking rationally. I was being bullied and I knew he could carry out threats like taking the children away from me. He told me many lies and repeatedly said that no one in church cared about me and over a period of time I began to half-believe his lies. The psychological abuse has been massive and expressed in so many different ways. There were times when I had suicidal thoughts and felt depressed.*

Q: Eventually, you had no choice but to separate from and then divorce your husband. Can you share a little about this?

A: *How does one describe a separation and divorce? Embarrassment and a feeling of shame were very real coupled with a sense of isolation. All my expectations of a happy and God-honouring marriage had evaporated. Often, I woke up in the mornings in a sweat and panic, feeling despair. I felt that I stood out like a leper and people were not sure what to do or say to me, even in church. I never expected when I married that I would ever become divorced and consequently a single mother. It was extremely difficult to adjust and relate to people generally, including those in church, because of my circumstances. Not deliberately I know, but we were often left out of social occasions when some church families met for a picnic or an outing.*

Q: In probing how pastoral support can be improved, can you specify pressure points and areas where you needed and would have valued genuine and practical support?

A: *I'll refer to a few instances where support would have been appreciated.*

1. One pressure point was collecting the children from their father on pre-arranged times of access as there were regular battles and abuse on these occasions. It may have helped if someone else had been with me or had gone in my place at times.

2. It was necessary to go to Court on many occasions to ensure custody of the children and gain a Court Order. Here was a huge pressure point; I was scared and returned home in shock and feeling exhausted. To have had regular physical support from a trusted friend may have helped, although I know some were concerned and praying for me.

3. I would have valued more practical help such as a rota of friends sharing with me the burden of taking the children to and from schools, including after-school activities and also children's meetings in church.

This would have eased my burden considerably if help had been consistently available, as I was also often physically unwell.

4. One woman encouraged me to phone her at crisis points when I needed to talk. That was a great help and I valued it. Others did it too or texted me in concern and love. This can be encouraged in a church.

5. What I am really saying and calling for in churches is **a support network**. I see this as a protective network being put in place by the church, but wisely and sensitively. What I would like is for two ladies in a church whom I can trust and who also understand my situation, to form this protective network. The ladies would be wise, understanding and mindful of the issues but able to keep confidentiality. One of whom could be available 24/7, especially if I found myself in a crisis or in danger. Perhaps a chat on the phone would be adequate at times but on other occasions they may need to come to my home or for us to meet in a neutral place. Such a network would be a major part of a recovery process. I cannot overestimate its value but the network has to be 'involved' in the on-going mess! Wherever there are victims of domestic abuse, this kind of support network would be invaluable both to the victim and the children.

6. I plead with pastoral leaders to accept victims of domestic abuse, whatever the circumstances, and show them practical love and concern, but not pity! Perhaps pastoral leaders in a local church can also set an example by drawing a victim and their children into their own family or other families for a meal or just fun and relaxation during the week or at the weekend. With my children I have often been kept out of church families, perhaps unintentionally, but we have longed to be accepted and welcomed, especially where there were other children in the same age bracket.

Q: Thank you for these suggestions but there is one final question. In the Lord's providence, you are now in recovery mode and more encouraged in your situation. What has helped you during this continuing recovery process?

A: *Obviously much less contact with the abuser has eased the problem, and the texting is much less now, though related to the children; however, he abuses me psychologically whenever he has the opportunity. The impact of the abuse has been considerable over the years and it will take time to undo the damage. Counselling has helped with support from civil agencies. Church support is helpful, especially specific individuals who have shown love and understanding. But the Lord has given me grace and strengthened me, keeping me when I felt hopeless, helpless and worthless. To Him be the praise for His amazing grace. I now want to be used of the Lord in encouraging hurting women who are, or have been, in similar circumstances. There is a great need in society and in our churches.*

In addition to Elen, Louise, Isabella and Vera now offer their suggestions for improving the pastoral care of victims of domestic abuse. Vera's experience of pastoral care, however, was extremely positive and we can also learn from her experience.

2. Louise
Louise has shared her own personal story earlier but now offers her perspective as a victim in suggesting what action can be taken by churches to protect people in abusive relationships. She offers five suggestions:

i) *Gospel*
'Teach the Gospel. We are broken men and women living in a broken world. God is a God who rescues us. He forgives and restores. Make sure that this message is heard clearly. Divorce is not the unforgiveable sin. If we have sinned, we have a Saviour who has died for us'.

162

ii) *Careful in teaching*

'Be careful how you preach. Teach the whole picture. Yes, women should submit to their husbands, but men should also love their wives like Christ loved the church. We need to hear more of this!'

iii) *Servant leadership*

'Men should model servant leadership. Don't allow any kind of bullying from men or women to go on in your churches. Model loving and kind relationships. This will help put up a mirror, revealing to victims of domestic abuse that the way they are being treated in their homes is unacceptable. Create the right culture in your church.'

iv) *Don't jump in!*

'Don't jump in with telling people to be reconciled. We should forgive but pushing people to move from this to reconciliation shows that you are under-estimating the damage caused by abusive relationships and the danger.'

v) *Keep safe*

'Keep your women safe. Encourage and assist them to leave dangerous relationships.'[1]

3. Isabella

Isabella is a member in the Anglican church in Australia and was married to a clergyman who abused her for years. Her remarks in this respect are few but important.

When a wife separates from her husband who happens to be a clergy-man, the congregation is often not informed of the real reasons for the couple separating or leaving the church. The church allows 'a cloud of ambiguity to form as to what was going on in the marriage. No impression was given that any serious transgression had occurred.' The

---

1   Email correspondence October 2017.

downside of this for the wife is that she is deprived of any 'potential support' she may have received from the congregation. 'The cloud frequently forms over the wife's reputation but allows the abuser to escape without the appropriate consequences ...'

There are huge challenges to churches in this statement by Isabella. Openness on the part of church leaders, for example, in informing the congregation concerning the reason for a marriage break-up in their fellowship is really important, and more especially if it is a leader. Again, another challenge is to ensure that the victim is cared for prayerfully and practically by the church and not isolated from her/his friends. Isabella also asks churches to discipline and care for the abuser appropriately rather than covering up his abuse and allowing him/her to continue in the church or another church, sometimes in a leadership position.

4. Vera

Churches are often criticised for a lack of love and concern for victims of domestic abuse. Often the criticism is justified and, as we have seen, more needs to be done in extending care to those coping with abusive partners. There are, nevertheless, churches where victims are loved and protected. That was the experience of Vera. And churches can learn from her story.

Relief

It was a great relief to Vera when her pastor believed and understood her suffering in an abusive relationship. She was even more encouraged when he informed her that he was deeply concerned about her emotional wellbeing. The pastor also advised her to make a note of the incidents of abuse occurring in the home while at the same time to have a bag ready with essentials in case she had to leave the house in an emergency, especially if she feared the violence was becoming dangerous.

Encouraged

Other factors too encouraged Vera in her church. There was the pastor's assurance that she could phone him or his wife at any time, night or day, and they would take her to their home initially for safety. That was a huge encouragement. Vera feels valued by the pastor and others in the church. She is not regarded as a nuisance or a 'problem' case.

Protected

Again, the pastor did not believe she should stay in the marriage at all costs, despite what the abuser did to her. Panic feelings overwhelm her when she anticipates her husband attending their church service. That will be a shock but the church has promised to protect and support her even in that situation.

Thrilled

What thrills Vera further is that the church people cope with her mood swings. There are days when she feels happier but other times when she is overwhelmed by flashbacks which make her feel frightened and desperate. Guilt and self-hatred only add to her confusion yet the church people are there for her, whatever. The church is not perfect as Vera would acknowledge but she knows the church loves and cares for her, and that she is on a long journey with its many twists and turns – she needs the Lord to be with her, but also His church.

PART B: SUGGESTIONS FOR PASTORING DOMESTIC ABUSE SUFFERERS: CHURCHES/AGENCIES

In this section of the chapter, we turn from the suggestions given by victims to draw on a sample of recommendations for pastoral care from churches and specialist charities working with individuals suffering domestic abuse as well as the abuser.

The chronological order of these samples has no ecclesiastical or other significance!

1. *First, the* Fellowship of Independent Evangelical Churches *(F.I.E.C) offers some basic advice to church leaders*[2]. High on their list of priorities concerns the need for the preaching and teaching in churches to address frequently issues relating to domestic abuse, indicating that such abuse is unacceptable and contrary to God's Word. Another priority is for a church, where possible, to have a female pastoral worker. Abused women are often afraid of approaching a male leader for help whereas the female pastoral team member may be more approachable and less daunting.

There is also the helpful recommendation for pastors to discuss the issues relating to domestic abuse in their Ministers' Fraternals. If done occasionally, this can be mutually informative and keep the issue within their radar. Other recommendations include being prepared to face this pastoral challenge, even though there may be no known instance of it currently in the church. Related to this is the recommendation to prepare, in addition to a child protection policy, safeguarding procedures or a Church Charter [3] suitable for those experiencing domestic abuse. Further recommendations suggested by the FIEC are that all church 'members, including Sunday School teachers' and youth leaders should be 'cautious' in not 'emphasising too much' obedience to parents, teachers and adults lest they be taken advantage of. The church needs to be alert to signs that abuse may be going on.

2. *A second sample of pastoral advice comes from the Church of England, namely, their document:* Responding to domestic

---

2   *Christian Citizenship Bulletin*, Issue No.52, November 2002, p.27.

3   *Restored: Ending Violence Against Women: A Pack for Churches* provides a helpful example of a Church Charter, 37; www.restoredrelationships.org

abuse: Guidelines for those with pastoral responsibilities[4].
Here we find numerous suggestions and recommendations,
some have already been referred to. With regards to helping
a victim, pastoral workers are urged to talk in a safe place,
take ample time to listen and believe what is being said rather
than being judgemental. One should ask about the children
and whether they are witnesses and/or abused themselves.
Confidentiality is again emphasised but alongside a warning
not to confront an alleged abuser or offer to mediate. No
pastoral worker should make decisions for the abused person as
they can change their minds frequently. Nor should we expect
decisions in a hurry because 'leaving may be as frightening as
staying' for the abused person. A recommendation is given to
help the abused individual to make a contingency plan which
can make them feel in control of their life.

Four further aspects in these Guidelines deserve mention as
being very important:

One aspect concerns ***those from a minority background***
who suffer domestic abuse.[5] In churches where immigrants
and asylum seekers attend church meetings, the following
Guidelines need to be respected by church leaders:

- Build a sense of security and trust.
- Take extreme care before deciding whether family or
  community support networks would be beneficial – they
  may be part of the problem.
- Make referrals, where possible, for support and advice
  to organisations from the same background but with a
  reliable track record of helping domestic abuse victims.

---

4   Church House Publishing, London, 2006. This Document acknowledges the
    research on domestic abuse received by the 2002 Methodist Conference in
    England; it also refers to the 'comprehensive report' called *Taking Action: Domestic
    Abuse and the Methodist Church* which was received by the 2005 Methodist
    Conference.

5   *Responding to Domestic Abuse: Guidelines*, p. 12.

- If asylum seekers are involved, it is wise to refer the problem to specialists and recognised agencies.
- Continue to befriend and support the individual (and children), remembering the isolation, shame and poverty which may befall women from different ethnic backgrounds.
- Do not attempt to reconcile or mediate out of respect for cultural differences for this can place the survivor at further risk.

A second aspect touched on in this document is *'the abuse of humility'*. This will be discussed further in the next chapter with regard to marriage and relationships within the church, yet points made here deserve mention. An opening statement is: 'While theologies of domination have had a pernicious effect in encouraging abusive behaviour by men, the corrective, a theology of humility, has often been misapplied to women, increasing the imbalance between the expectations of each sex held by churches and societies. It has been forgotten that Jesus' teaching and ministry not only humbled the exalted but exalted the humble.'[6]

For any survivor or abuser who compares the suffering involved in domestic abuse with the suffering of the Lord Jesus Christ and Christian disciples or martyrs, a three-fold response is provided:

- The sufferings and death of the Lord were unique and redemptive whereas Christians and martyrs willingly embrace suffering, even death, as part of their discipleship and expression of love to the Lord. It does not follow that victims of domestic abuse should continue in abusive relationships either to suffer like Christ or the martyrs.

---

6   *Responding to Domestic Abuse: Guidelines*, p. 19-20.

To argue that their suffering abuse may have redemptive value in changing the attitude of an abuser, is misguided.

- In a related way, our Lord lovingly embraced the most awful sufferings in order to save us. He did so willingly and freely. Christian martyrs also freely laid down their lives for the Lord but in domestic abuse, a victim is frightened and battered into submission and oppression. There is no real freedom for the victim.

- A clear distinction is necessary between genuine self-denial which is involved in Christian discipleship and submission to abuse. Suffering abuse of any kind is contrary to God's revealed will in the Bible so such suffering is not genuine self- denial.

A third aspect in these Guidelines which requires mention here is that of ***children who witness domestic abuse.***[7] This is now regarded as a crime. But too often children are the forgotten victims of domestic abuse. Miriam's story in an earlier chapter highlights their needs and the extent of their suffering. Children in these circumstances are vulnerable because they can be physically hurt in protecting their mother or feel frightened by what they witness. One child I knew well, and who had a long-term illness, felt her father was violent towards her mother largely because he did not like her being ill. The child was convinced of this and it took time to persuade her otherwise. Children in similar circumstances will be scared of the abuser, often resulting in bed-wetting, being clingy, depressed and over-anxious. It is not uncommon for a child to be reluctant to go to school in a desire to protect their parent. They are often more aware of the problem than parents realise and long for them as parents to love and care for one another.

---

7   *Responding to Domestic Abuse: Guidelines*, p. 31-34.

Pastorally, the suggestions below – some of which were mentioned earlier, are important:

- Interaction with church families, especially children their own age, can be helpful.
- If the abuser has left the home, one or more trusted and caring members in the church can assist with school-runs, homework, leisure activities and relaxing with the children.
- If the domestic abuse is deemed serious, and affecting the child/ren adversely, then the church's Child Protection Policy should be applied.
- In church activities for children and young people, officers can have useful opportunities to talk informally with children and identify possible needs and problems.
- An appropriate person from outside the family who will listen to their worries and seek to help them.

3. A third and final sample of pastoral advice is one of several charities specialising in helping women in domestic abuse situations. I refer here to *RESTORED,*[8] which is 'an international Christian alliance working to transform relationships and end violence against women', working in over twenty-five countries. The origins of the charity go back to 2008 when Mandy Marshall and Peter Grant heard the stories of women who were being abused in their homes by men. They were challenged by two questions: 'where is the church' and 'where are the men' who can assume responsibility and seek to prevent violence against women? That was why they established *Restored*, believing that *'Christian churches have huge potential to help prevent violence, but we also need to change our own attitudes and practices.'*

---

8   www.restoredrelationships.org

A pack is available for churches under the title, *Ending Domestic Abuse* which is extremely informative and includes a Church Charter on the subject with a Church Self-Assessment Tool. They list the '4Rs' of responding to domestic abuse which are:

Recognise: abuse occurs in Christian relationships and signs of it are power and control in the relationship.

Respond: believing the victim is a helpful response and respond within your limitations and the safeguarding framework.

Refer: to the National Domestic Violence Helpline–0808 2000 247 and do not hesitate to refer to local professionals.

Record: dates and what is said with any action taken or concerns you may have.

In the next chapter we turn to consider marriage within the context of an abusive relationship.

ACTION POINTS

1. What can pastors and church elders do with their members to improve the pastoral care of abuse victims?

2. Are there suggestions you find more helpful and relevant to your situation?

12. Husbands and Wives: An Abusive Relationship

Our discussion of marriage will be within the framework of conflict and domestic abuse in a contemporary context. First of all, we identify four different models of marriage before turning to discuss specific 'flashpoints' in the marriage relationship which victims of domestic abuse have identified as being problematic, often intolerable.

MARRIAGE: FOUR MODELS

For approximately five decades, attitudes towards marriage in the United Kingdom, have changed radically. This is also true in the United States of America and other countries. Post-war societal changes with the emergence of secularism then feminism have led increasingly to different approaches to marriage. Following the liberalising 1960s, the second wave of feminism in the early 1970s tended to assume a traditional heterosexual and nuclear-family model yet within a more egalitarian understanding of the roles of husband and wife. By the 1990s, the increasing divorce rate, the growing acceptance of co-habitation alongside the gay lobby and gradual increase in same-sex relationships further weakened traditional marriage. The third wave of feminism from the 1990s emerged as it sought a more radical approach to marriage[1] which included

---

1   *Manifesto: Young Women, Feminism, and the Future,* Jennifer Baungardner & Amy Richards.

either its elimination or radical transformation. Within this social context, Christians have been influenced in varying degrees concerning their view of marriage and the 'traditional' view of marriage has become somewhat dated. The four models of marriage we are identifying in Western society are the following:

There is an *authoritarian and hierarchical model.* This model emphasises the submission of the wife to a husband who is the 'boss' and in complete control of the relationship. Submission is viewed as being the primary role of the wife and she may have little or no say in decision making. While this model may appeal to Ephesians 5:22-24, it fails to understand its radical, gracious context and emphasis on love. Too frequently in cases of domestic abuse, whether for unbelievers or believers, this is the model the abuser follows. It represents a harsh, unrelenting and cruel approach. Church leaders need to demonstrate from Scripture and from their own marriage relationships that this model of marriage is unacceptable.

The second model is *complementarian* which the author favours as being the more biblical model. Here, both husband and wife are equal in the sight of God but with different gifts and roles. The husband is called to lead but importantly to love his wife 'as Christ loved the church'. The wife responds in submission to her loving husband while both share responsibilities and privileges within the relationship and family. The wife is in no way inferior to the husband.

A third model of marriage which is more popular is the *egalitarian model* where both partners are completely equal in their roles and share joint leadership; the headship of the husband in the relationship is rejected. Submission is understood as being mutual (Eph. 5:21).

The fourth contemporary marriage model is the *revisionist model* which includes shades of differing radical attitudes towards marriage. It goes well beyond the egalitarian model by either questioning the institution of marriage itself or questioning the permanence of the marriage relationship while allowing same-sex partnerships. However, this model is extremely diverse in its attitude to marriage yet all share a radically revisionist approach.

MARRIAGE: SPECIFIC 'FLASHPOINTS'

The rest of this chapter explores biblically specific flashpoints in the marital relationship, flashpoints which are common in domestic abuse situations and yet also feature in varying degrees in other marriages. For that reason, you will not find an exhaustive treatment of biblical teaching on marriage or divorce in this chapter, although a few helpful resources will be referenced for those wanting to read further.

What is distinctive about this section is that it identifies major flashpoints from the experience of victims of domestic abuse. This has involved listening to the stories and desperate cries of victims, reflecting on questions relating to their turbulent marriage relationship and – often – its termination, as well as observing the emotional, physical impact and 'damage' of the abuse on their lives and families. From the descriptions provided by Christians concerning their experience of domestic abuse, four areas are highlighted independently by them all, namely, the lack of respect shown them by the abuser, the absence of genuine love, an oppressive and unbiblical emphasis on submission and the issue of divorce. The themes of respect, love and submission are major Bible emphases intended by the Lord to dominate all human relationships and not just that between a husband and wife. While listening to the cries of victims in relation to these areas, the Bible will be our absolute authority in all areas of faith and behaviour.

A. Respect: 1 Peter 3:7

'Husbands, likewise, dwell with them with understanding, giving honor to the wife, as to the weaker vessel, and as *being* heirs together of the grace of life, that your prayers may not be hindered .'

> *...there was not a single day without verbal, psychological and physical abuse – often violently, sometimes using objects like a knife ... he has shown no respect at all for me over the years (Rita).*

> *... he would often throw things at me... (Louise).*

> *he always criticized everything I said or even how I laughed. This he usually conveyed after people had gone or by the angry way he'd look at me when they were still there.*

> *Sometimes he'd call me out of the room to tell me off, or in some cases tell anyone who was with me to go away as he wanted to speak to me alone ... a broken nose, a bruised face, and knocked unconscious at least twice ... he used to pick me up and throw me ... kick me ... he hit me so badly that I had to leave in a hurry ... (Charlotte).*

> *I felt trapped in my marriage ... I lived in fear ... My opinions or feelings did not count at all. He showed me no respect (Jane).*

Those perpetrating the abuse above are husbands and professing Christians, some of whom were church leaders. Interestingly, after devoting six verses in 1 Peter 3 to encouraging wives regarding holy living and submission to their husbands, the apostle Peter refers briefly but 'forcefully'[2] and practically to husbands concerning their marital responsibilities. Edmund P Clowney observes: 'The path of Christian living is no different for the husband than for the wife. Both are called to follow Christ in humble and compassionate love, accepting rebuffs

---

2   Grudem, W *The First Epistle of Peter,* (Leicester: IVP, 1988), pp. 142-146.

with forgiving grace (3:8-9).'[3] This statement to husbands in verse seven can easily be missed so your attention is drawn to its four-fold message as one way of considering the importance of respect within any relationship, especially marriage.

'Understanding'

Notice first that husbands should live with their wives 'with understanding' or according to 'knowledge'. This means that husbands need to understand the divinely given instructions for marriage in the Bible and treat their wives accordingly. Rather than express anger, indulge in outbursts of temper which often include verbal, psychological and physical abuse, a Christian husband's relationship and attitude to his wife must reflect submission to Christ's lordship.

'Honour'[4]

We notice secondly that this 'knowledge' relates to 'giving honour to the wife, as to the weaker vessel'. The 'giving of honour' is an important theme in the New Testament. God himself is pleased to bestow honour on those who are weak, sinful and despised by the world (1 Cor. 1:26-30, James 2:5, 4:6 and Matt. 5: 3-12). Similarly, rather than abusing his wife, a husband should 'bestow honour' on her which will include kindness, respect, support and sensitivity. This is particularly important because the wife is 'the weaker vessel' in terms of physical strength; she will in most cases also be emotionally more sensitive and vulnerable. Paul has this aspect in mind when in Colossians 3:19, he instructs husbands to 'love your wives and do not be bitter (or 'harsh') toward them[5]. Wives

---

3   Clowney, Edmund. P. *The Message of 1 Peter* (Leicester: IVP, 1988), p. 133.

4   Clowney, 134 (where Clowney emphasises that here 'respect' is an inadequate translation).

5   Husbands often '*use harsh language with their wives. They treat them with a severity that others would find offensive if they could see it. This bitterness clearly fails to reflect the tender and faithful affection with which Christ loves the church*'; http://www.ligonier. org/blog/husbands-warning- against-bitterness/

need to be honoured and cared for rather than abused. Clowney reminds us that 'Peter uses the same word which in 2:7 is translated as 'precious'; literally it does mean 'preciousness'. The honour or preciousness that the husband must bestow on his wife is not only the recognition of her place in God's ordinance of marriage; it is the honour that is hers as one of God's precious and holy people.'[6]

'Heirs together'

Another reason for a husband honouring his wife is that they are 'heirs together of the grace of life'. This has far reaching implications for the marriage relationship, again commanding respect from the husband. Both husband and wife are equal before God as joint-sharers in divine grace with all the benefits of their union with Christ and adoption. The wife is in no way inferior spiritually but frequently may be more intelligent, prayerful and godly than her husband. Here then is a further reason for the husband to show respect to his wife and enjoy rich fellowship together with the Lord in the Word and prayer. Their roles are different but importantly they are 'heirs together of the grace of life' as they trust and serve the Lord.

Prayers 'hindered'

There is a final reason given to husbands why they should honour their wives. A failure to do so on the husband's part will mean that his prayers will be 'hindered' by God as part of his fatherly discipline of his children (Heb. 12:3-11).This is 'a strong word'[7] and the passive mood of the verb indicates that it is God who acts in interrupting His relationship with a husband – or any believer – if he is not living in an 'understanding' and loving way with his wife. No husband, whatever his church position, can expect answered prayers

---

6   Clowney, p. 134-135.
7   Clowney, p. 135.

unless he lives in a loving and biblical way with his wife, showing honour and respect. The following practical pointers, therefore, are relevant:

- Prayer ought to be central in a marriage relationship with the wife and husband praying together daily, honestly and humbly.
- A husband's prayers will be 'blocked' by the Lord and lose their 'effectiveness' if he fails to 'honour' his wife as the Bible directs.
- Prayer is empty and false if there is not a close, loving relationship between husband and wife. After all, this marriage relationship was designed by God to mirror the love of Christ for the church, and of the church for Christ.'

B. LOVE: 'HUSBANDS, LOVE YOUR WIVES...' EPHESIANS 5: 25-33

In the church I am now a member of, and love, men are often called to be leaders in their homes. However, I have never heard them called to love, cherish and honour their wives, and I have listened hard to hear this. (Louise)

I felt desperate and bitterly disappointed for marriage was not what I imagined it would be like and instead of loving, my husband was critical, unkind and cruel. The marriage was a sham. (Rita)

... despite all the abuse in the home, I still loved the man who abused me and the children, even despite my fears and desperation – but he did not show us any love ... (Lucille).

Context

Victims of domestic abuse claim there is a lack of balance in many churches regarding teaching and understanding the roles of a husband and wife. While the wife's submission may sometimes be highlighted, yet in the context of Ephesians 5 and the rest of the New Testament this is only one strand in what is rich, comprehensive teaching on the subject. This wider context can be illustrated in numerous ways.

One of the ways of appreciating the wider context is to give due weight to Ephesians 5 verse 21: *'submitting to one another in the fear of God'*. This strong statement enforces what was said in the preceding statements with the word *'fear'* carrying the ideas of reverence, awe and loving respect. For Christians, Jesus Christ is the Lord who expects loving obedience from His people. As Lord He rules over believers by His Word and Holy Spirit. Therefore, it is not a matter of whether we like other people or agree with them or feel inclined to respect them, for the responsibility of Christians without exception is to submit graciously to others, expressing grace, kindness and holiness in all relationships and situations. The motive is to please and obey Christ in all our relationships, and not only in the marriage relationship. Therefore, we should not read verses 22-24 in Ephesians 5 without grasping the message of verse 21. Glenda Hotton endorses this in reminding wives that 'the issue is not really submission to our husbands: it is submission in general. If we took out God's command to wives to submit to their husbands, we'd still have to deal with his command to "be subject to one another in the fear of [Christ]" (Eph. 5:21).'[8]

To feel the full force of verse 21, notice that a participle is used emphasising a continuing activity; therefore, all believers are to be 'submitting (or being subject) to one another' all the time and in all relationships. It is not the wife alone who is expected to submit; rather, humility and graciousness

---

8   Hotton, Glenda *Help! I Can't Submit To My Husband*, (Leominster, England: Day One Publications, 2012), p. 15.

should be expressed by both men and women in **all** their relationships. This obviously includes husbands, whoever they are and whatever positions they hold in a church. Only after this general exhortation to submission does the specific call for the wife to submit to her husband follow. This sequence is vitally important and will be developed later. But how often in churches are all Christians called upon to express and fulfil this submissive and gracious attitude towards one another?

Another way of appreciating the context in Ephesians 5 is to notice the heavier responsibilities placed upon the husband in verses 25-31. Only three verses are devoted to the wife yet treble that number of verses are directed to husbands, so victims of domestic abuse are correct in referring to an imbalance often in the church's teaching. The husband's role and his responsibilities are pivotal, yet too often more attention is given to the wife's role of submission.

'Love'

The context can be pursued further by underlining what is expected of husbands: 'love your wives, just as Christ also loved the church and gave Himself for her...' (verse 25). That is an impossible standard of course for we cannot love as He loved. However, Christ's love for His church imposes on husbands an obligation to love their wives as Christ loves the church. Charles Hodge affirms that 'Christ's love is held up as an example and a rule.'[9] His love is exclusive, unselfish, kind, sacrificial and purposeful. Here is a huge 'counter-cultural'[10] challenge for Christian men not to be preoccupied with their own needs, desires or whims but rather consider the needs of others first, especially the wife. In underlining this crucial

---

9   Hodge, Charles *A Commentary on The Epistle to the Ephesians*, (London: Banner of Truth, 1964), p. 315.

10 Gardner, Paul *Ephesians: Encouragement and Joy in Christ*, (Fearn, Ross-shire: Christian Focus, 2007), p. 147.

point, Western Christians must recognise their danger of regarding 'love' mostly as an emotion rather than an action. There is no doubt that in the Bible the emphasis is on love as being active. As many as two hundred or more verses in the New Testament include the word 'love' and its cognates yet strikingly, only three references relate to the love between husband and wife, but the verb used each time indicates action.

The apostle Paul continues to argue and persuade husbands in this passage to fulfil their role of loving their wives in a Christ-like way. For example, just as a man cares instinctively for the needs of his own body 'so husbands ought to love their own wives as their own bodies ...' (verse 28). The point is a telling one. But the apostle's argument is taken further in verses 29-30 by repeating 'just as the Lord does the church. For we are members of His body, of His flesh and of His bones'. What do we learn here? I may love my wife for many reasons but the ultimate reason for doing so is Christ Himself. After all, as a Christian husband I am a member of Christ's church and am being nourished, cared for and protected by Christ. How amazing is the love of Christ to each member of His church in dying for them, then continuing to care for them until one day they will be completely holy and without blame in glory. This is unconditional, sacrificial, eternal and incomparable love. And as a husband I am the recipient of this love so I need to be more like Christ in loving and caring for my wife unconditionally, unselfishly and sacrificially. Avoiding an abusive, violent, hateful, selfish, prideful, tyrannical male domination, the Bible calls husbands to a 'Christ-like, selfless, sacrificial, male headship/leadership' in marriage.[11]

There is even more to excite Christian husbands here. A deep union exists between a husband and wife involving

11   *The Peaceful Wife*, April Cassidy, Blog, July 4, 2015.

physical union alongside an intimate knowledge of one another. This however is only a pale reflection of a more profoundly intimate, spiritual and eternal union between Christ and His church (verses 30-33) which Christian marriage is intended to reflect and point to. Christian husbands need to wake up to this teaching and to love their wives as Christ loved the church. There is no place for unkindness, cruelty, hurtful words and attitudes towards one's wife, whatever the circumstances may be and however provoked an individual may feel. [12]

C. SUBMISSION: 'WIVES, SUBMIT TO YOUR OWN HUSBANDS, AS TO THE LORD...' EPHESIANS 5:22-24

it's not for you to think, it's for you to do – submit and obey... I became a 'doormat', only doing things at his behest. (Charlotte)

submission in marriage involved for me complete, unconditional obedience, however unreasonable. (Lucille)

I was told that my duty was to obey ... you're submissive, you ask permission to do things and that was my life. (Jane)

My clergy husband became more rigid and emotionally dominating. He did not like dominant women and wanted to see them submit. He used force during arguments like grabbing my neck or placing his hand over my mouth and nose—he said I deserved it because I had raised my voice and shown contempt. I had not shown submission. (Jess)

I believed wives should always submit to their husbands. I felt very guilty when I did not want to do something my husband asked of me. (Louise)

These examples can be multiplied. Those clergy wives in Australia who spoke to 7.30 and ABC NEWS, for example, claimed that the teaching of submission was a major factor

---

12 Some helpful and practical points are made on this aspect by Jeremy Bailey in *What does the Bible really say about..? MARRIAGE* (Leominster, DayOne Publications, 2017), p. 15-21.

in contributing to their domestic abuse and Ephesians 5:22-24 was normally used by their husbands in demanding submission.

Relevant considerations

In responding to the misuse of the 'submission' principle illustrated above, there are numerous considerations which must be highlighted if we are to understand the Bible's teaching on 'submission' correctly; these considerations are pivotal in grasping this biblical principle of submission.

1. Inseparable

One immediate consideration is that the responsibilities of husband and wife are inseparably related in a profound, harmonious unity; to isolate them is not only unbiblical and dishonouring to God but also disastrous for the marriage relationship. We dare not speak therefore of the wife's submission to her husband without referring to, and demanding, the husband's exercise of his leadership role in a Christ-like loving manner. Submission, authority and love are inseparable and not mutually exclusive.

2. Trinitarian

Secondly, Natalie Brand is right and biblical in placing this important point within a trinitarian context when she writes:

The wife's voluntary submission to her husband affirms his authority in leadership and love. We consider authority with love and not merely the duty of 'authority' or 'headship' as other complementarians outline. In this male-female order established in the taxis of the triune Godhead who 'is love' (1 John 4:7-8) and dwells perichoretically in perfect love, love should not be marginalised. When authority and love and submission are seen together, these biblical codes make perfect sense.[13]

---

13   Brand, Natalie *Complementarian Spirituality: Reformed Women and Union with Christ* (Eugene, Oregon: Wipf & Stock, 2013), p. 118.

No Christian husband is entitled to ignore his responsibility to love his wife; any exercise of his leadership and expectations of his partner's submission must be tied inexorably to the need for him to love.

3. 'a gracious cascade'

Thirdly, this trinitarian consideration can be developed further as it is foundational to an understanding of submission in marriage. For example, there is no inequality in the intra-trinitarian relationships; the Father, Son and Holy Spirit are each co-equal, co-eternal and co-substantial. Consider the eternal love between the Father and the Son for 'there is a very definite shape to their relationship... The Father's love is primary...'[14] and in that love he sends and directs the Son. From 1 Corinthians 11:3, Michael Reeves emphasises that

> *the shape of the Father-Son relationship (the headship) begins a gracious cascade like a waterfall of love: as the Father is the lover and head of the Son, so the Son goes out to be the lover and the head of the church... That dynamic is also to be replicated in marriages, husbands being the heads of their wives, loving them as Christ the head loves his bride, the church... Like the church then wives are not left to earn the love of their husbands; they can enjoy it as something lavished on them freely, unconditionally and maximally... Christ so loves the church that he excites our love in response; the husband so loves his wife that he excites her to love him back.*

This perspective can transform relationships, including marital relationships.

4. 'supreme example'

A fourth consideration is necessary. The verb *'submit'* in verse 21 is rightly assumed to govern Paul's exhortation to wives

---

14 Reeves, Michael *The Good God: Enjoying Father, Son and Spirit*, (Milton Keynes: Paternoster, 2013), p. 10.

in verses 22-24. In verse 21 the word 'submit' has the basic meaning of being under other people and this is confirmed in Colossians 3:18 and 1 Peter 3:1-6.

A practical question arises as to what submission involves in relationships with other people, including the wife in relation to her husband?

The wider context of Ephesians 5: 21 is profoundly challenging in this respect. From Ephesians 4:17-5:20 the apostle makes clear that those who have been born again and redeemed by Christ and indwelt by the Holy Spirit, must live differently. Their transformed thinking and desires (4:17-18, 20-23) must be expressed in avoiding immorality (4:19) as they seek to be more like the Lord (4:24-29) in turning from sins like lying, bitterness, theft, bad language, rage, slander and malice.

By contrast, kindness, compassion, a forgiving attitude and modelling their lives on the example of Christ's sacrificial love are the qualities which should characterise the lives of ALL Christians (4:31-5:7). This is part of what it means to walk in the light (5:8-14), in wisdom (5:15-21) and in love (4:31-5:7. In other words, it is people who live like this who are 'submitting to one another'. It is not the wife alone, therefore, who submits. A humility and graciousness should be expressed in all our relationships, including husbands as well as all other believers. Only after this general exhortation to submission does the specific call for the wife to submit to her husband follow. This order and sequence is vitally important.

I concur with Paul Gardner that Philippians 2:3 'provides the most complete summary of what this submission will be like'[15] in terms of a genuinely humble, submissive attitude in which others are more highly regarded. The supreme example

---

15   Gardner, Paul *Ephesians: Encouragement and Joy in Christ,* (Fearn: Christian Focus, 2007), p. 143.

of humility, love and submission to his Father's will that Paul provides is that of the Lord Jesus Christ (Phil. 2:5-11). Those who love Christ and are manifesting the 'fruit of the Spirit' (Gal. 5: 22-26) will not abuse other individuals, and certainly not their wives.

5. Headship

A final consideration is relevant at this point; wives submit to their husbands for two other important reasons which are summarised succinctly by John Stott: 'The priority of Adam's creation established his headship (1 Tim. 2:13) ... while Eve's folly in challenging it led to disaster (v.14).'[16] The first reason can be amplified a little. While Adam was created first thereby establishing male headship, Eve was intended as 'a helper comparable to him' (Gen. 2:18). This does not refer to, or imply, an inferior status but rather it denotes a difference of function. For example, the woman was necessary for fulfilling the cultural mandate of Genesis 1:28: 'Be fruitful, and multiply, fill the earth ...' She, not the man, has the ability to procreate. Again, Adam needed a close, intimate relationship with Eve to be able to function adequately. Her role was to partner her husband in serving and honouring the Lord together. There is no suggestion of inferiority in her status as a wife for she is 'a helper' and partner 'comparable' to him. In practice this means that both minor and major details concerning the family and their own lives are discussed and shared before reaching decisions. The partnership approach is honoured.

Misunderstandings

From these relevant considerations we now highlight below some popular misunderstandings of what this submission looks like in marital life:

---

16 Stott, John *The Message of 1 Timothy & Titus*, (Nottingham: IVP, 1996), pp. 86-87.

- It does not mean agreeing with everything the husband says or decides!

- Submission does not demand that the wife remains passive and fearful of giving an opinion and advice.

- A husband is not infallible. In fact, he can be unwise, suggesting responses and actions which could be inappropriate, even foolish. A husband may even want his wife to do something contrary to God's Word. If so, a Christian wife must refuse and say, 'We ought to obey God rather than man' (Acts 5:29).

- Submission to a husband does not exclude exchanging ideas frankly, discussing options and challenging respectfully a decision a husband is considering or is inclined to make.

- There may come a point however, even after prolonged and helpful discussion, that a basic disagreement exists. At that point, Ephesians 5 verse 21 applies either in the husband deciding not to go ahead without mutual consent or the wife submitting to the husband's leadership, even though she may be unhappy with the decision.

- Nor does submission mean a universal submission of women to men; rather it is the submission of a wife to her own husband.

- A wife's submission is never intended in the Bible to become slavery or oppression. Nor should a wife or husband feel unsafe and frightened in marriage.

- The submission required in the Bible is not a cold, clinical response but a heart attitude governed by God's grace in Christ. No husband can create such a heart attitude in his wife. His primary task is to love his wife as Christ loved the church. His example in loving his wife will encourage a genuine and loving submission from her.

W.G.N. Martin summarises the biblical teaching helpfully:

> ... *in many things, for example, spiritual qualities, the woman is the natural (and divinely ordained) equal of man. But in the relationships of family life, God has ordained a certain order ... This subordination does not imply inferiority ... The husband must find the pattern of his conduct in the conduct of Christ towards His church ... no oppression, but self-sacrifice ... Paul emphasises not rights but responsibilities ...* [17]

Angry

Emily is only now rediscovering her faith after suffering years of abuse from her husband. She was only too aware that her husband had failed miserably to pattern his life and behaviour on 'the conduct of Christ towards His church ...' As a consequence, she suffered extensively from abuse. Emily writes:

> *I was so furious at the advice of Christian leaders over the years to rejoice in suffering and to be content ... I could not read the Bible verses on submission because they made me angry ... My husband had told me I must submit to, and obey, him, but he ignored his responsibility to lay down his life for his wife ... submission in a marriage is not about dominating or demanding servitude; the gospel is not about being a law keeper. It is about grace, and a man – Jesus – who laid down his life for his enemies. It is about showing love to people who are broken, and so I always try to come back to that.* [18]

By way of contrast, the following example illustrates how this teaching has been worked out in two Christian marriages:

Example 1: John and Noel Piper

17 Davidson F (ed) *The New Bible Commentary* (London: IVP, 1954), pp. 1028.

18 *Raped, tracked, humiliated: Clergy wives speak out about domestic violence*, 7.30 and ABC NEWS, Australia. 23 November 2017.

John Piper refers to his own marriage relationship in an attempt to illustrate how as a married couple they faced the question of a wife's submission:

> *If you asked my wife, 'What does submission look like for the Pipers?' one thing she would say is, 'We settled the principle early that if we can't agree, Johnny's going to make the call'. That's really basic. And it almost never happens. One of the reasons it almost never happens is that we've been together a long time, and we know what each other thinks. Another important reason is that I often yield to Noel. I don't need to be right, or to have my own way, or to have the last word.*[19]

Example 2: Timothy and Kathy Keller

It is Kathy Keller who has written a chapter in her husband's book, *The Meaning of Marriage*[20] in which she shares some of the principles which guided them as a couple in their 'everyday decisions as well as our more complicated decisions. These guidelines', she affirms, 'have proved useful to us …'

One major principle is that the 'husband's authority (like the Son's over us) is never used to please himself but only to serve the interests of his wife (Rom. 15:22-3). A servant-leader must sacrifice his wants and needs to please and build up his partner (Eph. 5:21ff).'

The **second** principle identified is that 'a wife is never to be merely compliant but is to use her resources to empower. She is to be her husband's most trusted friend and counsellor, as he is hers (Prov. 2:17). The "completion" that embracing the other involves a lot of give and take … need to hear each other out … involves loving contention (Prov. 27:17) … until you sharpen, enrich and enhance each other …'

---

19 Https://www.desiringgod.org/articles/*six-things-submission-is-not,* February 26, 2016.

20 Keller, Timothy *The Meaning of Marriage: Facing the Complexities of Commitment with the Wisdom of God,* (London, Hodder & Stoughton, 2011), p. 241 ff.

The **third** principle she shares is that 'a wife is not to give her husband unconditional obedience', for reasons we have already noted.

A **fourth** principle receives much more attention for the reason there is 'the most misunderstanding ...' The principle is: 'Assuming the role of headship is only done for the purpose of ministering to your wife and family ...'

How does this work out in practice? The answer is challenging: 'a head can only overrule his spouse if he is sure that her choice would be destructive to her or to the family.' While the husband 'does not use his headship selfishly ...' YET 'the wife will try to respect her husband's leadership, and the husband will in turn try to please his wife. If this dynamic is in place, in the course of a healthy biblical marriage, "overruling" will be rare.'

What happens when a couple disagree? '... this should be the place where the one the Bible calls "head" takes the accountability. Often an intelligent husband doesn't want this role and the intelligent wife does! The situation could be chaotic, but here we are called to act out the drama of redemption, where the Son voluntarily gives the headship to the Father, saying, "Not my will, but thine be done."'

Kathy Keller then illustrates the point with regard to her husband's decision in the late 1980s to move to New York to lead a church plant. As a family they were happily settled in Philadelphia where Tim was a professor. Whereas her husband was excited over the prospect of this new challenge, Kathy was 'appalled' and expressed her 'strong doubts' to her husband. His response was gracious and conciliatory: 'if you don't want to go then we won't!' Kathy was horrified and replied, 'No ... You aren't putting the decision on me ... if you think this is the right thing to do, then exercise your leadership ... It's my job to wrestle with God until I can joyfully support your call.' The rest of the story is history as the Lord prospered his ministry in New York.

These two examples are helpful in many ways. Both couples are honest in acknowledging that there were times when as married couples they disagreed although each wife submitted to her husband's decision. That is far from easy, and for some it is always difficult!

Again, there was no stubborn insistence on having one's own way or long-term resentment, either by the wife or the husband. Here is a reminder that adjustments need to be made by both partners as they get to know each other in a developing relationship of trust, love and shared understanding of their respective responsibilities. Submission in marriage, therefore, has nothing to do with power, cruelty and abuse. Furthermore, the above examples remind us that marriage is a partnership with both partners being equal yet with different gifts and interests. Their mutual love and respect for one another prompts and motivates them to cooperate and complement one another in the relationship yet the final leadership role lies with the husband. For that reason, marriage is a learning curve for both partners. Not infrequently, the wife is more gifted, earning more than her husband which may necessitate the husband shouldering more responsibility in caring for the home and the children.

In the next chapter we will consider the issue of divorce; victims of domestic abuse are requesting clarity and guidance in churches concerning the Bible's teaching on this subject.

ACTION POINTS

1. Which model/s of marriage do you recognise from reading this chapter?

2. Identify questions or difficulties you have concerning the teaching on submission.

3. Is prayer central in your marriage and in your life? Have you considered previously that the Lord sometimes 'hinders' the prayers of husbands if there is a wrong attitude towards one's wife?

13. Husbands and Wives: Divorce?

In the previous chapter we identified four different models of marriage before exploring three flashpoints in the marital relationship which are common in domestic abuse situations and can also feature in varying degrees in other marriages. Four areas were highlighted independently by Christians concerning their experience of domestic abuse, namely, the lack of respect shown them by the abuser, the absence of genuine love, and an oppressive and unbiblical emphasis on submission. The fourth 'flashpoint' related to divorce. Having considered three of these flashpoints, we now turn to the fourth one, the vexed question of divorce; is it biblical for domestic abuse victims to divorce?

DIVORCE?

Is it biblical? I wrestled with the question of divorce...I was confused whether it was biblical or not. But there was no other way out for me and the children … (Mary)

There was little choice in the end but to separate and divorce … It was very difficult for a sheltered Christian to be thrown into the world of divorce with the associated legal wrangling … The worst aspect of it all, however, was the betrayal and deceit by someone I had really thought would be my rock … (Charlotte)

I did not believe divorce was permissible, so I had to keep going ... The subject of divorce does not seem to be preached in our churches, apart from a condemning way. The church I go to does not appear to have a clear view of when divorce is valid ...

I still believe God has designed marriage to be a lifelong commitment between a man and a woman. But if only this is taught, with no clear teaching on divorce or acknowledgement that sometimes in our broken world divorce is better than staying in a damaging, threatening and dangerous marriage, then it leaves people like myself trapped ...

I ask, what does the Bible really teach on the subject of divorce? (Louise)

PRESSING QUESTION

In addressing this pressing question, the focus majors on domestic abuse victims, male or female. All the victims I have met and corresponded with are Christians who have honoured their marriage commitment for years, despite suffering abuse. They even feel guilty discussing, or recalling, their own separation and divorce. Legally, they are entitled to pursue the divorce option but their question is whether the Bible permits it. Or should they remain in an abusive, often dangerous, relationship, honouring their marriage vows at all cost? That has been the pastoral advice significant numbers of victims have received from church leaders.

DISAGREEMENT: AMERICA

Churches and church leaders disagree concerning the question whether, if at all, divorce is legitimate, even for victims of domestic abuse, and this often creates confusion as well as feelings of guilt for victims.

A contemporary illustration from America illustrates the point. Generally, pastors there are more inclined to accept divorce where there is domestic violence, although 'almost half of American evangelicals (46 per cent) say divorce due to abuse is sinful' with '29 per cent of evangelical pastors in agreement'.[1] One 2017 Survey revealed that 59 per cent of pastors were inclined to 'believe divorce may be the best decision' if a church member filed for divorce on grounds of domestic violence. As many as 60 per cent affirmed they would 'investigate whether domestic violence is really present' with Lutherans, Methodists and Presbyterian/Reformed pastors more likely to believe such claims rather than Baptists and Pentecostals.

Consider then the response of a key leader in the Southern Baptist churches, Paige Patterson, president of Southwestern Baptist Theological Seminary in Texas, who has consistently held the view that divorce is wrong under any circumstance. 'I have never in my ministry counselled anyone to seek a divorce, and that's always wrong counsel', declared Patterson. However, he acknowledges 'an occasion or two when the level of the abuse was serious enough that I have counselled temporary separation and the seeking of help'. In fairness to Patterson, he affirms: '... I have never been abusive to any woman ... I have never counselled or condoned abuse of any kind. I will never be party to any position other than that of the defence of any weaker party when subjected to the threat of a stronger party. This certainly includes women and children. Any physical or sexual abuse of anyone should be reported immediately to the appropriate authorities, as I have always done.'[2] He adds a statement that has been misunderstood: 'God often uses difficult things that happen to us to produce ultimate good. And I will preach that truth until I die'.

---

1   2015 Survey: LifeWay Research. 'Good intentions, lack of plans mark church response to domestic violence. https://blog.lifeway.com/newsroom.2017/02/20good-intentions Last accessed 8 November 2018.

2   https://baptistnews.com/article/sbc-leader-under-fire-for-comments-about-divorce-abuse/#.WugBehbTXYX , 30 April, 2018.

The bottom line however is that he has never suggested or encouraged divorce because he considers it to be unbiblical.

But is it unbiblical in some circumstances to obtain divorce, as Patterson maintains? If so, are domestic abuse victims therefore imprisoned within a cruel abusive relationship until they die? What does the Bible teach? That is the question we are addressing in this section, but first a brief word about the victims.

Anguish

It is in confusion and desperation as well as in feelings of guilt that victims wrestle with the divorce question in an abusive marriage. They know heartbreak and disillusionment because their expectations for a loving and God-honouring marriage have been smashed into pieces. Their marriage vows were made on the understanding that only death would part them. The Lord's words reinforced the fact that marriage was for life: '...what God has joined together, let not man separate' (Matt. 19:6). More than likely the Lord was referring here to marriage as a creation ordinance rather than to individual marriages, but either way victims have wanted to honour this creation ordinance and follow God's instructions for marriage. Consequently, their sadness and guilt feelings are profound before, and long after, a divorce.

Explore

In answering their question concerning divorce, there is no intention to be controversial or dismissive of other views. Nor is there any attempt to provide easy answers for those trapped in abusive marriages. Some readers will disagree with my conclusions but if I stimulate readers to consider even more seriously the biblical teaching on the subject then I will be encouraged, whatever conclusions are reached. I am sharing here the fruit of my own wrestling with the subject. One thing is certain. The issues of divorce and remarriage will not go away so here is an attempt to explore the subject briefly but sensitively and biblically, with regard to domestic abuse victims.

Principles

Without referring in detail to the broad sweep of biblical teaching on divorce or pursuing in-depth exegetical discussion of key texts, the aim here is only to suggest an answer to the questions of victims which is grounded in basic biblical principles.

These principles include the unity of the Old and New Testaments with no genuine contradictions in the Bible's teaching. Progressive revelation, too, ensures that the Old Testament provides essential background to, and finds fulfilment in, the New Testament. The flow of biblical revelation also involves giving attention to the immediate as well as the wider contexts of statements on divorce. For example, one cannot jump directly from Genesis 2:24 to Matthew 19:4-5 or to 1 Corinthians 7 while ignoring what is written between those statements. Again, the Lord Jesus in the Gospels and Paul in 1 Corinthians 7 are responding, without contradiction, to different situations and their teaching is consistent and complementary.

What must also be recognised is that in Matthew 19:6 and Mark 10: 2-9, the Lord, for example, was answering a specific question hotly debated between two groups of Pharisees, namely the Hillelites and Shammaites. They fiercely disagreed regarding the phrase '*any cause*' in Matthew 19:3. The latter adopted a strict interpretation that divorce was allowed only for serious sexual sin while the former and more liberal group understood Deuteronomy 24:1 to permit divorce for trivial reasons.

Influence

Protestants have been influenced significantly by Roman Catholic and Anglican teaching on the subject of marriage and divorce. Due initially to Augustine's influence, the Western Church assumed that marriage is permanent and should not be dissolved, whatever the circumstances. Gradually the Roman Catholic Church understood marriage as a sacrament so that a valid marriage should not be dissolved. Both Anglicanism and Nonconformity in varying degrees have been influenced by this high view of marriage. Divorce tended therefore either to be forbidden, restricted to adultery alone or strongly discouraged and frowned upon in churches. By contrast, it is assumed here that the Bible's teaching on marriage/divorce is firm but compassionate and realistic in recognising that sin ruins marriages and families. Divorce in some circumstances is biblical.

Grounds for divorce

The position suggested here is that the Bible permits divorce in cases of adultery/fornication as well as desertion/separation with the latter including, for example, domestic abuse situations:

1. **adultery/*'fornication'*:** Matthew 5:32, 19:3-9; Deuteronomy 24: 1-4

Where one partner is unfaithful sexually with a third party, the innocent partner is free either to initiate divorce or to remain in the marriage. Some may want to seek counselling in order to preserve the marriage and restore, if possible, a relationship of trust. This latter approach is consistent with what the Lord teaches in the Gospels and the apostle Paul in 1 Corinthians

7. They both start their teaching by discouraging divorce in strong terms and Paul also emphasises in this context the principle of reconciliation (1 Cor. 7:11). However, adultery is a ground for divorce in the Bible.

Realistically, two observations can be made at this point. The first is that adultery is sadly becoming a common reason for married couples seeking divorce. The interplay of contributory factors here is complex but marriages can be too easily and quickly entered into while extra-marital relationships are a feature of contemporary society with its amoral lens. Too often the example of friends, even relatives, who divorce can provide, even unconsciously, an escape route for other couples when the going becomes challenging. The second observation is that Christians are not exempt from these influences and trends. Here again is highlighted the urgent need for at least Christian couples to be prepared by church leaders pastorally and biblically for the responsibilities and privileges of marriages.

Returning to the ground of adultery for divorce, there is considerable debate concerning the significance and application of the Greek word *porneia*[3] often translated as '*sexual immorality'* in the above references and also in 1 Corinthians 6:9 and 1 Timothy 1:10. While the word includes adultery, I assume it has a wider application,[4] for example, to homosexual acts, indecent exposure, indulgence in pornography and the sexual abuse of children.

2. desertion/separation: Exodus 21:10-11; 1 Corinthians 7:15

---

3   Clark, Stephen *Putting Asunder: Divorce and Remarriage in biblical and pastoral perspective,* (Bridgend, Bryntirion Press, 1999), see pages 49-109 and 110-136 for a detailed discussion of this word and its implications.

4   Hamer, Colin *God's Divorce: Understanding New Testament Divorce and Remarriage Teaching,* (London, Faithbuilders, Apostolos Publishing, 2017), p. 136.

In considering this ground for divorce, we can obtain an historical perspective by referring to a major Protestant statement on the subject, the Westminster Confession of Faith (WCF): 'nothing but adultery, or such *wilful desertion* as can in no way be remedied by the church or civil magistrate, is cause sufficient of dissolving the bond of marriage.'[5]

While the WCF teaches that adultery is a biblical ground for divorce, the inclusion of the word *'or'* may refer to desertion as an additional basis for divorce distinct from adultery/fornication. The words *'wilful desertion'* emphasise the deliberate nature of those who leave their marriage partner with no intention of returning. A. A. Hodge endorses this statement: 'The only causes upon which it is lawful to grant a divorce are: (a) adultery; this is explicitly allowed by Christ (Matt. 5:31-32, 19:9) and (b) wilful, causeless, and incurable desertion ... allowed by Paul to the Christian husband or wife deserted by their heathen partner (1 Cor. 7:15).'[6]

Observations

Some brief observations are necessary here. First, Hodge appears to go further than the WCF by introducing the word *'causeless'*, suggesting there may be no specific or satisfactory reason for the desertion. Two, where there is desertion it is assumed rightly that attempts will be made by a pastoral leadership or a civil authority/agency to effect reconciliation. The WCF, however, acknowledges that in these circumstances the point may be reached when the relationship 'can in no way be remedied' and this realism is necessary in the complexity of human relationships. Three, one cannot interpret desertion only as abandoning the marital home; rather it is the marriage itself which is being abandoned. Four, the term 'desertion' as

---

5   *The Confession of Faith,* Chapter XXIV; Section VI: Marriage and Divorce.

6   *The Confession of Faith: A Handbook of Christian Doctrine Expounding The Westminster Confession,* A.A. Hodge (London, Banner of Truth, 1958), p. 307.

used by the WCF requires more elasticity in interpreting and applying it. Hodge assumes like many that the desertion is by a 'heathen partner' but this is questionable. For example, in a domestic abuse situation the victim, whether wife or husband, is often driven from the home and the marriage relationship by years of physical and psychological abuse. I concur with Paul Brown's conclusion[7] that this is 'equivalent to divorce. No-one can be expected to stay in a situation in which they are exposed to continual violence' and abuse yet it is the abuser who has driven the victim away. Desertion is not the most appropriate word to describe victims of domestic abuse on leaving the marital home and seeking divorce. The point will now be made biblically.

Biblical

What does the Bible teach about divorce for abuse victims? Here I share a little of my own journey in grappling with the biblical data regarding this question and I suggest some key points for your consideration:

1. The Old Testament teaching on divorce has generally been neglected in studying the subject. Some readers may be surprised that the Old Testament should be relevant here but, as indicated earlier, it is part of God's Word and underlies, and then is amplified, in the New Testament. What is also important is the big picture or meta-narrative in the Bible which embraces the Old and New Testaments. In referring to Scripture's marital imagery, Colin Hamer writes: 'God asks us to *imagine* that he is married to his people, or as it is in the New Testament, that Jesus is the bridegroom of the church. A central theme of this imagery, which runs from Genesis to Revelation, is God's own divorce and remarriage.'[8]

---

7   Brown, Paul E. *Christian Marriage*, (London: Grace Publications Trust, 2014), p. 71.

8   Hamer, p. 9.

This may sound strange to some. However, the point is illustrated in God's covenantal relationship with Adam, our federal head, which resembled a marriage; Adam and Eve were driven from the Garden when they sinned. They were unfaithful. At Sinai, a new covenantal relationship was established with Israel but the later Assyrian then Babylonian captivities were understood as a divorce from God due to their unfaithfulness over long periods, which involved the rejection of God's Word and messengers as well as their daily disobedience to the Lord. Nevertheless, Jeremiah (31:31-33) and other prophets proclaimed a remarriage in the future to be fulfilled in the coming of Jesus Christ the bridegroom (John 3:28-29). By the bridegroom's incarnation, life and saving work, He redeemed his bride, pledging to take her home to heaven purified, then finally to ensure their participation in the marriage supper of the Lamb (Rev. 19:6-9). Here is the rich biblical canvas against which we view the exciting dealings of God with His people, but it is expressed biblically in marital imagery and in terms of 'God's own divorce and remarriage'.

2. We should not be surprised therefore that lying behind the Lord's statements in Matthew 5:32, 19:3-9 and Paul's teaching in 1 Corinthians chapter 7 are key Old Testament texts like Exodus 21:10-11 and Deuteronomy 24:1-4. The Exodus text in 21:10-11 is relevant, for the wife is recognised as having conjugal 'rights', including sexual intercourse but also clothes, food and emotional support or loving care. If the husband failed to provide these rights then this constituted grounds for the wife to initiate divorce from her husband. Nowhere in the New Testament do we find that our Lord's teaching in the Gospels changes that provision.

3. The Lord Jesus in Matthew 19: 1-7 allows divorce where there is 'adultery' or, more widely, 'sexual immorality'. However, a further question arises here. Should we **also** understand the word 'adultery' metaphorically in line with the Bible's own marital imagery? Colin Hamer, for example, suggests 'it is more likely Jesus is speaking metaphorically – that is, Jesus is using the term "adultery" in the way it is used in the Bible's marital imagery.' [9]

In support of this view, Hamer refers to the way in which the Lord sometimes described the people in His day metaphorically as an *'adulterous generation'* (Mark 8:38). We should not dismiss this interpretation lightly, especially because of the marital imagery used to describe God's relationship with His people in the Bible. There is no suggestion on this occasion that the Lord thought that the people were committing physical adultery but, consistent with the Old Testament teaching, He accused them of being unfaithful to their covenant God; they were covenant breakers and disobedient. That is precisely what the prophets had accused Israel of in the Old Testament. If this metaphorical interpretation is acknowledged as being biblical and providing the 'big picture' then the reference to 'adultery' could be wider than sexual unfaithfulness, including unfaithfulness by husbands in failing to love, care for and respect their wives as required in the Word.

4. 1 Corinthians 7 – relevant pointers meriting consideration when discussing divorce:

- A high view of marriage as a creation ordinance is acknowledged by the Lord in the gospels and by Paul in 1 Corinthians 7, alongside a strong discouragement of divorce. This is apparent in 1 Corinthians 7 where he is applying the Old Testament teaching on divorce and remarriage to the New Testament church. In Matthew 19:3 the Lord rejects the Hillelites liberal view that divorce was available for minor and selfish reasons.

---

9   Hamer, *p.* 108.

Here is a warning that on biblical grounds we dare not sanction divorce in **all** circumstances.

- As we have already noted, the Jewish background coupled with the Old Testament Scripture provide the framework for the apostle's approach to marriage in this chapter, despite addressing a church in the Graeco-Roman world. Earlier points made about the Old Testament texts and biblical marital imagery must be the lens used for reading this chapter.

- The opening verses of 1 Corinthians 7 are foundational for understanding the chapter and the biblical teaching on divorce. **Verses 3-5**, for example, appear to be based on Exodus 21:10 where the responsibilities of the husband towards his wife are repeated.

- This principle from **Exodus 21:10** relates also to a marriage partner who refuses to engage in sexual union and thereby refuses to consummate the marriage. An earlier chapter provided details of a husband whose wife refused sexual intercourse for nearly five years of marriage and then agreed to it for a brief time only because she wanted children. The husband did not want to annul the marriage because he loved the woman. Clearly her attitude was unbiblical (1 Cor. 7:5, Eph. 5:28-33, Heb. 13:4). This unhappy situation in which the wife also increasingly 'controlled' the relationship in other ways led eventually to divorce –and, I suggest, on biblical grounds!

- In **verse 8**, Stephen Clark argues that 'the unmarried' referred to here included those who had been divorced, possibly before their conversion.[10]

- The apostle turns in **verses 10-16** to issues of separation and divorce. The language is strong, confirming the

10   Clark, p. 145.

Lord's teaching that from creation divorce was not the divine intention. In **verses 10-11**, therefore, this general principle or *'command'* is underlined so neither husband nor wife should seek divorce. It is almost certain that the Lord's *'command'* referred to here is **Mark 10:12** where the Lord refers to a woman not leaving her husband. Nevertheless, immediately in **verse 11** of 1 Corinthians 7, Paul qualifies the principle in discussing those who do 'separate'. Paul is introducing what Clark calls 'pastoral realism'[11] in which the Bible's teaching on marriage is not realised. While marriage should be honoured and preserved, wherever possible, nevertheless Paul recognises realistically that in some situations separation may be necessary and wise; if there is separation, however, then reconciliation should at least have been sought.

- Whatever the final outcome may be, we are reminded that *'God has called us to peace'* (1 Cor. 7:15), implying that counselling and encouragement to restore the relationship are appropriate until reconciliation appears impossible. Here Paul is qualifying the general principle he has underlined in acknowledging that reconciliation is impossible in some situations. Such a person is *'not under bondage' or 'enslaved'*[12] – a phrase which is variously understood. I suggest that both statements involve a deserting wife (or husband) and in effect divorcing the partner, so being free consequently to remarry.

- **Verses 39-40** are usually considered as insisting on the permanence of marriage; it is an indissoluble relationship unless one partner dies. I question this understanding of the verses. Firstly, the context is different, because

---

11   Clark, pp. 149-150.
12   Hamer, pp. 242-243.

from verse 25 the apostle is discussing 'virgins' or those betrothed to be married and he is giving them advice. This point is significant so that verses 39-40 conclude this brief section from verse 25. Secondly, Paul acknowledges there were challenges facing betrothed couples. For example, in that the church faced a critical situation, might marriage for such couples impose too heavy a burden for one or the other? This may be in mind at the end of verse 28. Thirdly, the challenges facing a betrothed couple are referred to again in verses 36-38, but the verses are difficult to understand. The man who feels it appropriate to marry the lady he is betrothed to, should do so and does not sin. Or the alternative is for the man to wait for a while before marrying his betrothed. In verses 39-40 it is the betrothed woman who is in view. She is betrothed to the man as long as he lives, that is, until a decision is made to proceed further to marriage yet it would be within a reasonable and restricted length of time.

In this section we have cited some key biblical statements on marriage and divorce, suggesting that there are biblical grounds in some circumstances where divorce is legitimate. These circumstances relate to: 1) a wife not being cared for, loved, provided and cared for by the husband; 2) sexual immorality outside marriage by the wife or husband then 3) desertion by one marriage partner.

You are encouraged to consider these points further. However, I make one plea. Give careful thought to what the Bible teaches on divorce and be persuaded that you are really conveying God's Word to survivors of domestic abuse who feel the desperate need to separate and divorce their partner.

The next chapter concludes our wide-ranging consideration of domestic abuse.

ACTION POINTS

1. Reflect on the principles and approach adopted in this chapter to consider the Bible's teaching on divorce.

2. Do you agree with the grounds for divorce suggested in this chapter? Give reasons for your answer.

14. Conclusion

On completing this book on the contemporary challenges concerning domestic abuse, three dominant thoughts are in my mind.

1. REQUEST

I am only too aware that I wrote this book at the request of some victims/survivors of domestic abuse. I was moved by learning of their sad experiences but also their desire for me to go public by speaking and writing on the subject. Domestic abuse for them was not a mere discussion subject or contemporary phenomenon which was gaining publicity and Government support. They themselves had suffered abuse and rather than looking on as spectators, they care voluntarily for others in similar circumstances in their localities and churches.

Some helpful books and articles have been written on this subject but this book belongs to the survivors, for it is their stories, their concerns and their recommendations which constitute the heart of this book, making it distinctive and useful. Running through their stories is their concern for women in similar circumstances and still alone in them. To these women I dedicate this book.

2. LOCAL CHURCH

A second dominant thought has gripped me in completing the writing of this book, namely that so many victims of domestic abuse have been let down by their churches and leaders. That is sad. While I was aware of the failure of some churches to pastor victims, I was surprised by the extent of this failure in the United Kingdom. My sense of surprise may be regarded as naïve, but I reply that my biblical view of the church really contributes to my surprise.

Let me explain. A local church is the creation of the gospel, indwelt by the Holy Spirit, governed and equipped by the Lord Jesus Christ. By means of the preaching of the gospel and the regenerating work of the Holy Spirit, men and women are brought as sinners to trust and obey the Lord Jesus Christ. It is such people, from different backgrounds, circumstances and ages who meet together and constitute the church within a locality. The Lord rules His people by the infallible Word of God and the Holy Spirit; He also appoints pastors and elders to teach and rule in accordance with the Bible.

There is much more to be said about the church but I confine myself to two points. The church is the unit established by the Lord where believers enjoy fellowship, receive pastoral care and serve Him. Christ, the only head of the church, has instituted the preaching of the Word, baptism, the Lord's Supper, prayer, godly conversation and fellowship as a means whereby He strengthens, instructs, comforts, sanctifies, preserves and revives His people. The ministry of pastor and elders provided by the Lord is for the purpose of 'feeding the church of God' (Acts 20:28 and Eph. 4:11-18). The church therefore is central in God's purpose.

This being so, there are implications for churches with regard, for example, to pastoring abuse victims of any kind. Think about it for a moment.

Christians are called to be *'light'* and also *'salt'* in the world (Matt. 5:13-16) and to live godly, compassionate lives in society. Another implication is that God is righteous (Deut. 32:4) and His righteous standards include protection for weaker members of society like the poor, orphans, widows, the sick, abused, slaves and migrants; they all require compassion and respect (Lev. 19:9ff). Church discipline may be in order in dealing with some perpetrators, in addition to legal action and formal restraints.

A further implication is the need to support governments in restraining evil and promoting what is good (Rom. 13: 1-7) and to pray for them (1 Tim. 2:1-6). This is relevant as the United Kingdom Government is currently pressing forward with additional measures to address domestic abuse.

A final implication is that Churches and individual Christians are entrusted with the Lord's gospel of love – a love which must be shared with everyone, including survivors of domestic and other forms of abuse. Love must be extended to all, irrespective of status, gender, age, need, ethnicity, lifestyle or location (Matt. 22:37-40; Mark 12:28-34): *'wholehearted love for God means coming to see other people as God sees them, and all people as the objects of God's love'*[1].

Can we take Amy Carmichael (1867-1951) as a challenge to churches? Here is a Christian who expressed God's love for women and girls, then boys, in South India, seeking to rescue them from danger and prostitution. Amy became aware of Indian children, especially girls, being sold by poor families and dedicated to Hindu temples where they lived in moral and spiritual danger. Despite opposition and danger, Amy persevered in her work. Treasuring God's love in Christ, she expressed the divine love in practical, costly ways and like *'an overflowing pool of love–overflowing on others.'* Her words are:

---

1   Morris, L., *The Gospel According to Matthew*, (Leicester: IVP, 1992), p. 564.

'We have no love in ourselves, and our pools would soon be empty if it were not for that great, glorious, exhaustless sea of love'[2]. Churches are called in God's purpose to be an *'overflowing pool of love'* locally where they are, and among those to benefit from such love should be victims of abuse.

3. 'BIG PICTURE'

A final dominant thought also grips me as I complete this book, namely, the 'big picture' of God's dealing with the world. That is exciting, for the entire universe and its history are under the sovereign rule and care of the triune God (Col. 1:16-17; Dan. 4:35). This is God's world. He created it; it belongs to Him (Ps. 24:1).He sustains it and His glory is stamped upon creation, proclaiming His existence and 'eternal power' which 'are clearly seen' so people 'are without excuse' (Rom. 1:20-22) in their sin.

Unique

Humans are unique, too, because they are created in 'the image of God' (Gen. 1:26-27); it is God's will that all people be treated with dignity and their human rights honoured. However, man's historic fall into sin (Gen. 3; Rom. 5:12-21) spoilt our relationship with God, a disaster of cosmic proportions affecting, amongst other things, human relationships. The voice of conscience, though stifled and weakened, yet still speaks, even in acts of exploitation, murder, violence, abuse and other sins. That is only part of the big picture. God's redemptive purpose was accomplished by the Lord Jesus Christ in His perfect life and then at Calvary where He bore the punishment of our sin. This salvation is applied personally to the elect by the Holy Spirit, effecting a radical change in sinners who are brought to faith in, and union with, Christ to live under Christ's lordship.

---

2   Murray, Iain. H., *Amy Carmichael, 'Beauty for Ashes', A Biography,* (Edinburgh: Banner of Truth, 2015), p. 135.

An ongoing work of sanctification in believers is guaranteed by divine omnipotence, ensuring they live transformed lives, forming the new and redeemed God-centred humanity. That is not the end either! Jesus Christ is the Creator, Preserver, and Ruler; He is also the One who reconciles all things in the cosmos and makes peace by His sacrifice (Col. 1:15, 17). He is the Creator-Redeemer whose mediatorial rule involves not only His resurrection, ascension to heaven and session at the right hand of the Father, but also His personal return in glory to consummate the divine purposes both for the church and the cosmos. The One who created, and now preserves, the cosmos will also make a new earth and heaven at His appearing in glory (2 Pet. 3). There is a tension between the 'then' and the 'now'. The promised Christ has come; salvation has been achieved by Christ at Calvary and in Him the kingdom of God has come powerfully. He rules now and He must continue to rule until He has put all enemies under His feet so the full consummation of the kingdom is awaited (1 Cor. 15). The final kingdom will be established suddenly and gloriously; it will be public, universal and perfect, whereas the present aspect of the kingdom is established slowly, inwardly and imperfectly in this world. The church therefore must be prepared to live within this tension (1 John 3:2, Rom. 8:19-25) in faith, love and in obedience. This big picture can stimulate churches to follow the Lord closely and to express love and care to all, especially those who are needy and abused in our fellowships.

Also available from Christian Focus Publications…

LARA WILLIAMS

TO

Walk

OR

Stay

Trusting God through
shattered hopes and
suffocating fears

To Walk or Stay

Trusting God through shattered hopes and suffocating fears

LARA WILLIAMS

Her marriage slowly deteriorated behind the facade of a happy, Christian home. After six years together, with three young children, Lara discovered the devastating reality of her husband's marital betrayal. Lara gives tender guidance to any woman walking the unexpected paths of betrayal. But even more than that, she testifies of the victorious life in Christ available to everyone, regardless of any shattered hopes or suffocating fears.

This is no mere 'winning-through' story. It is about how theology changes lives. It brings big doctrines into home and marriage and the choices we make every day. Very relevant and very good thinking.

Ann Benton
Author and family conference speaker

Lara Williams teaches and reminds her readers that we are not in control, but God is, and as we accept God's sovereignty and goodness, this radically changes how we view our relationship with Him, how we view ourselves, our circumstances, and how we view and relate to others.

Jane Tooher
Ministry Department, Director of the Priscilla and Aquila Centre, Moore Theological College, Sydney, Australia

978-1-78191-128-0

I AM MY SISTER'S KEEPER

Reaching out to Wounded Women

DENISE GEORGE

I am My Sister's Keeper

Reaching out to Wounded Women

Denise George

We live in a world of hurting women. And just as Jesus compassionately loved those who were suffering, so can we. 'As Christian women, our hearts ache with a world that suffers,' author Denise George cries. 'Our love for God compels us to put our love into action.'

I Am My Sister's Keeper tenderly addresses issues like broken relationships and divorce; unforgiveness; loneliness; spouse abuse; and loss and grief. Through biblical stories and contemporary stories of wounded women, George's advice guides readers in how to pray, offer a listening ear, share from their own experiences and encourage others with God's promises. A complete Bible study guide makes this an ideal resource for groups of women to study together.

Denise George writes from many years of experience of ministering to women. This book is faithful in portraying the reality of intense suffering in a fallen world, but equally faithful in presenting the resources for healing available to all in Christ. It will be a great resource for Christian women who are concerned to show Christ-like love to those who are suffering.

Sharon James
Conference speaker and author

978-1-84550-717-6

TRUTH AN

IN A **SEXUALLY** DISORDERED WORLD ♀♂⚥⚢⚣

AND LOVE

EDITED BY DAVID SEARLE

Truth and Love

In a Sexually Disordered World

EDITED BY DAVID SEARLE

Many people are confused about sex, morality and personal identity.

This book provides the background to distinctive Christian standards based on the Bible's teaching. It addresses the problems that you can encounter when seeking to encourage a Christ–commended lifestyle in today's society.

Contributors: David Wright, William Still, Geoffrey Grogan, David Searle.

An alternative title for this book might have been: Sex—handle with care! Sex has brought immense happiness to countless millions but it has also dealt sorrow and heartache to just as many. It need not, and it should not; hence this little book. In it the contributors present lucidly, and without need for apology, our Maker's instructions on how to handle one of the most wonderful gifts he has given to us—our human sexuality. If we will trust his guidance, we shall find it really is the way to lasting fulfilment and greatest joy.

William Philip
Minister, The Tron Church, Glasgow

978-1-84550-227-0

Christian Focus Publications

Our mission statement –

STAYING FAITHFUL

In dependence upon God we seek to impact the world through literature faithful to His infallible Word, the Bible. Our aim is to ensure that the Lord Jesus Christ is presented as the only hope to obtain forgiveness of sin, live a useful life and look forward to heaven with Him.

Our books are published in four imprints:

CHRISTIAN
FOCUS

Popular works including biographies, commentaries, basic doctrine and Christian living.

CHRISTIAN
HERITAGE

Books representing some of the best material from the rich heritage of the church.

MENTOR

Books written at a level suitable for Bible College and seminary students, pastors, and other serious readers. The imprint includes commentaries, doctrinal studies, examination of current issues and church history.

CF4•K

Children's books for quality Bible teaching and for all age groups: Sunday school curriculum, puzzle and activity books; personal and family devotional titles, biographies and inspirational stories – because you are never too young to know Jesus!

Christian Focus Publications Ltd,
Geanies House, Fearn, Ross-shire,
IV20 1TW, Scotland, United Kingdom.
www.christianfocus.com
blog.christianfocus.com